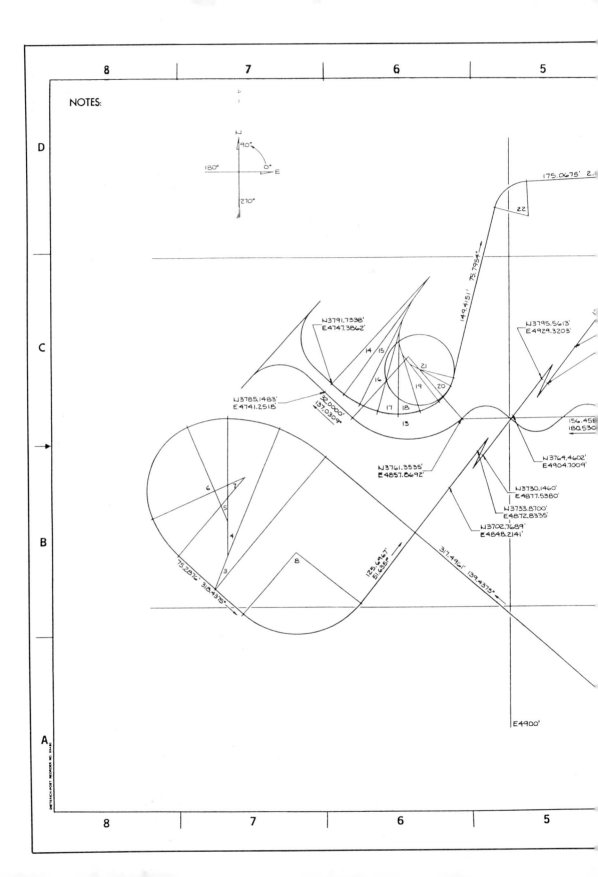

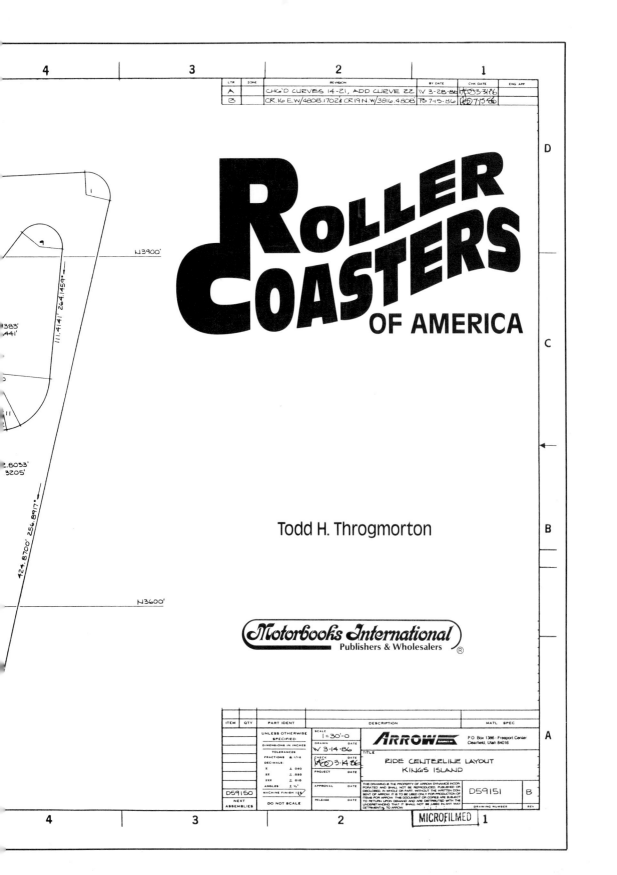

ROLLER COASTERS
OF AMERICA

Todd H. Throgmorton

Motorbooks International
Publishers & Wholesalers ®

LTR	ZONE	REVISION	BY DATE	CHK DATE	ENG APP
A		CHG'D CURVES 14-21, ADD CURVE 22	W 3-28-86		
B		CR 16 E.W/4808.1702 & CR 19 N.W/3816.4808	B 7-15-86		

ITEM	QTY	PART IDENT		DESCRIPTION	MATL SPEC	
			SCALE 1"=30'-0	**ARROW**	P.O. Box 1366 · Freeport Center Clearfield, Utah 84016	A
		UNLESS OTHERWISE SPECIFIED	DRAWN W 3-14-86 DATE	TITLE		
		DIMENSIONS IN INCHES TOLERANCES	CHECK 3-14-86 DATE	RIDE CENTERLINE LAYOUT KINGS ISLAND		
		FRACTIONS ± 1/16 DECIMALS: .X ± .060 .XX ± .030 .XXX ± .010 ANGLES ± ½°	PROJECT DATE			
			APPROVAL DATE		D59151	B
D59150		MACHINE FINISH 125	RELEASE DATE			
NEXT ASSEMBLIES		DO NOT SCALE			DRAWING NUMBER	REV

N3900'

N3600'

MICROFILMED

Dedication
For Susan and Samantha
And in memory of my mother who took me on my first roller coaster

First published in 1994 by Motorbooks International Publishers & Wholesalers, PO Box 2, 729 Prospect Avenue, Osceola, WI 54020 USA

Library of Congress Cataloging-in-Publication
    Throgmorton, Todd H.
      Roller coasters of America / Todd H. Throgmorton.
        p. cm.
    Includes index.
    ISBN 0-87938-929-X
    1. Roller coasters—United States. 2. Roller coasters—History.
    I. Title.
    GV1860.R64T48 1994   94-5341
    791'.06'8—dc20

On the front cover: Flashback at Six Flags Over Texas is one of the new breed of steel roller coasters. Built in 1985, it is designed to imitate flight.

On the back cover: Tornado at Adventureland is a classic-style woodie coaster, built in 1978. From a 93-foot-high lift, this 2840-foot-long coaster can reach 58 miles per hour during its 2-minute out-and-back run.

On the frontispiece: Riders hold their hands high as they round a banked curve on The Sky Princess, Dutch Wonderland's classically styled woodie roller coaster built in 1992.

On the title page: Arrow Dynamics' drafting analyzing the curves and arcs of Vortex, the steel-tube coaster at Kings Island.

Printed and bound in United States of America

Contents

Acknowledgments

I want to thank the amusement parks listed in this book for providing valuable historical information along with the photos of their roller coasters. Thanks also to the creative minds at Arrow Dynamics and Vekoma International who design and manufacture coasters for their informative assistance and photos.

In tracking down historic photos, the Museum of the City of New York, the Denver Public Library, the Library of Congress, Judith Walsh of the Brooklyn Public Library, Ann Parker with the Santa Cruz Beach Boardwalk and Susan Hormuth, an independent researcher, proved to be of tremendous help. To them I express my gratitude.

Finally, special thanks goes to my parents, Cuma and Sam, for the many hours spent at amusement parks all over the country, waiting for me and my brother Adam. It was at these parks that I became fascinated with the roller coaster. I became interested not only for the thrill of riding, but also for their historical background and the architectural presence of these great structures.

Todd H. Throgmorton

Author Todd Throgmorton, right, and his brother, Adam, with the working roller coaster model that Adam constructed.
Allen Photographics

The History of the Roller Coaster

*A*nticipation! Some call it fear; the feeling in the pit of your stomach as you slowly climb that long first hill, anxiously awaiting and imagining just what lurks beyond.

There is the slow creaking clickity-clack of the lift chain as it pulls you closer toward that first drop. As the train tops out, the passengers in the first few seats are dangled menacingly for a moment, allowing them one last look around at what will soon be a blur.

Then it happens. That sudden plunge as you fall like a rock, experiencing the "rush" that addicts you. From there the excitement of a series of dips and negative G-forces follows as you coast over the hills or of several high-banked fan curves that throw you from side to side.

This is a roller coaster!

The roller coaster is an American tradition, a part of our heritage, and in some cases, a link to the past. Maybe our parents or grandparents rode the same coasters that we ride today. The stories that can be told in recollection of those rides and the legends that are created are numerous. There may also be a celebrity connection to coasters such as aviation pioneer Orville Wright's fondness of the Coney Island Cyclone or the favorite of Elvis Presley, the Zippin Pippin in Memphis. However, in most cases, it is the roller coaster itself that has attained celebrity status.

*T*he roots of the roller coaster can be traced back to Russia in the late sixteenth and early seventeenth century. A Russian sport of this time was known as ice sliding,

Hold on to your hat!
Opposite page, this illustration appeared on the front cover of Frank Leslie's Illustrated Newspaper from New York, July 24, 1886. The subject was "Summer Diversions at the Seaside," with this "coasting" party at Coney Island. As the caption to the original noted, the riders were "more scared than hurt." Library of Congress

a winter recreation that was popular for nearly 200 years. Ice slides were first constructed by a Russian entrepreneur who discovered a basic principle that has become a foundation upon which the appeal of the roller coaster was built: People will actually pay to be terrified.

The concept behind the Russian ice slides was simple. A 70-foot wooden tower provided the initial starting point from where a 2-foot-long sled plunged down a ramp covered with ice. Each rider would sit on the lap of an experienced guide who steered the sled down the ramp and across a length of approximately 600 feet, coming to a stop at the base of another 70-foot tower. At this point the guide and his passenger would climb up the second tower to repeat the ride in the opposite direction, bringing them back to the original tower.

Due to their popularity, these ice slides could be found in cities and villages all over Russia, and the Russian royalty fancied the adventure. Ice slides near St. Petersburg were even strung with colored lanterns along the straightaway to provide for night sliding.

Of course, the ice needed to create an ice slide made the ride strictly a winter activity—until Catherine the Great had sleds fitted with tiny wheels so she could operate her ride during the warm months as well. This was the first of many refinements that would bring us the modern roller coaster.

In the late eighteenth century, a French traveler became fascinated with this unique Russian entertainment and took the idea home. The French adapted the ice slide to the milder Parisian climate by using a track made of closely spaced rollers, similar to a modern conveyer, on which sleds with runners could coast. This is the origin of the name roller coaster, a name which has endured even after the disappearance of coasting courses.

It was not long before the idea of replacing the sled runners with wheels took root. The first of these new recreational attractions made its debut at a public garden in the Ternes Quarter of Paris in 1804.

As the thrill became addictive, it inspired other French inventors to make improvements to the principle design. These new-fangled roller coasters appeared in picnic gardens throughout France much to the delight of the public. One such example was the Bellevue Mountains built in a Paris suburb during 1817. This coaster eliminated the need for climbing to a second tower for a return trip; instead, the sled simply gained enough speed down the first ramp to bring it up a second ramp, concluding at the top of the second tower where the ride repeated in reverse.

To take this idea one step further, a coaster named the Promenades Aeriennes made its debut as the first to allow passengers a return trip to their original starting point without stopping. The tracks were built in a circular form, and at the bottom of the initial drop, the track was banked so that the cars kept enough momentum to propel them up the incline and back into the station.

The Promenades Aeriennes coaster was chock full of innovations. In terms of safety, it was the first coaster designed with guide rails to keep the cars from jumping the track—an important attribute considering that these cars rounded the corners at more than 40 miles per hour, which was a considerable speed in the early 1800s.

The Promenades Aeriennes was also the first racing coaster. Two identical tracks ran side by side down the first 80-foot drop; at the bottom they split off, going in opposite directions. After completing the circular track, they came together again at the station.

This era of French coaster history provided a solid foundation from which to build, but for some unknown reason the French seemed to lose interest. The fad of the French "coasters" passed from fancy as quickly as it had arrived.

*T*he French contributions to fundamental roller coaster design should have been used to build upon, but the development of the coaster in America backtracked and these innovations were ignored until "discovered" or "invented" by American designers. For example, in 1826 a Frenchman by the name of Lebonjer patented a lifting device that would pull, via cable, the loaded coaster cars up the first hill; in fact, this is where the terms "lift hill" and "first drop" originated. The American coasters, however, did not incorporate the lift hill for several years. Regardless, it was the Americans who truly developed the roller coaster to its fullest potential.

The history of roller coasters in America is rooted in the mountains of Pennsylvania. The year was 1870 and an aban-

The French adapted the Russian ice slide to their milder climate by using a track made of closely spaced rollers similar to a modern conveyer on which sleds could coast. This is the origin of the name roller coaster.

doned mine train was converted to passenger use for sightseeing. The cars on the inclined railway were originally used to haul coal down to the village of Mauch Chunk from the top of Mount Pisgah in eastern Pennsylvania. With the help of horses, the train would be pulled to the top of the mountain to be loaded; with the horses then secured on board the train, it would make the return trip down a slight grade, which is said to have only dropped 60 feet to the mile.

The passenger version followed the same routine, with the people riding to the top and then enjoying the 6-mile-per-hour journey back. Named the Mauch Chunk Railway, people lined up by the hundreds for the privilege of riding, paying a nickel each. In fact, the ride proved so popular that the railroads even ran special trains to accommodate the attraction.

The success of the Mauch Chunk Railway led to the construction of "artificial coasting courses" similar to those in France. Like the French predecessors, the tracks were originally made of rollers, giving birth to the American name "roller coasters." As in France, wheels mounted on the cars soon replaced the rollers, but the name was firmly ensconced in American slang.

The first unique roller coaster to appear in America was the Gravity Pleasure Switchback Railway at Coney Island, which made its debut in 1884. Although similar in principle to its French ancestors, the new coaster was unique with its undulating track, earning the inventor, La Marcus Adna Thomp-

Coney Island Switchback Railway, 1884
Right, the Switchback Railway at Coney Island was a typical wooden coaster of its era. The cars were halted for this photograph as no camera of the time could catch them at speed. Library of Congress

son, the nickname "Father of Gravity." Thompson's ride in-cluded a series of gentle waves along a 600-foot-long track. Passengers sat sidesaddle to ride the wheeled cars, which reached top speeds of 6 miles per hour before coming to the end of the line. As with their predecessors, attendants had to push the cars up a second hill for the return trip.

Stories vary concerning Thompson's background and his ulterior motives in building the Switchback. One story refers to him as a Sunday school teacher from Philadelphia who wanted to divert young people from the popular beer gardens at Coney Island; another story credits him as a wealthy seamless hosiery inventor who saw an excellent business opportunity. Whatever the reason, by charging a nickel per ride, Thompson recovered his entire investment of $1,600 in just three weeks—to the utter amazement of his friends! This success inspired others to improve upon

Scenic Railway, circa 1900s
Above, the Mauch Chunk Railway was similar to the Cherrelyn Street Railway pictured above. The horse pulled the car and its riders in all of their finery up the hill to the peak, where the lucky horse was then loaded aboard, and the car swooped back downhill. This railway operated in Cherrelyn, Colorado, until 1910. Denver Public Library: Western History Department

his ideas, triggering a coaster construction boom. Thompson himself went on to build twenty-four more coasters in America and twenty in Europe, all exactly like his first.

Later in 1884, Charles Alcoke of Hamilton, Ohio, solved the "switchback" problem when he designed an oval track that returned passengers to the starting point, similar to the French Promenades Aeriennes. The phrase "out-and-back" was coined to describe the route of this track type. Alcokes' attraction, called the Serpentine Railway, achieved a top speed of 15 miles per hour while gliding over a series of mild hills and valleys.

Passengers sat sideways on these pioneering coasters until 1885 when Phillip Hinckle turned the seats forward with his new ride, the Gravity Pleasure Road. A native of San Francisco, Hinckle also introduced the idea of a steam-powered chain lift. With the combination of these inventions and refinements, an outbreak of coaster fever spread like a disease.

Scenic Railway, circa 1900s
Below, the L. A. Thompson Scenic Railway at the Santa Cruz Beach Boardwalk operated during the years 1908–1923. Historical File Warren Littlefield, Santa Cruz Seaside Co.

These improvements also meant that the Switchback coaster was obsolete, so Thompson decided to combine the new ideas with a few more of his own, creating the ultimate roller coaster of the era. The Oriental Scenic Railway, as it was called, opened in Atlantic City in 1886. On this ride, the loaded cars were automatically pulled to the top of the first incline before being set free to the force of gravity. It was patented as a "scenic railway," referring to the picturesque scenes of the Orient painted on the walls of lighted tunnels, which riders viewed halfway through the ride. Since that time, the United States Patent Office in Washington, D. C. refers to all roller coasters as scenic railways.

Once again, Thompson's idea proved so successful that he was swamped with order requests. As a result, the L. A.

Early Coaster Loop
Above, the Flip-Flap at Sea Lion Park boasted one of the earliest loops, which in turn was a natural sightseeing spot to watch the wonders of gravity unfold before your very eyes. Library of Congress

Early Coaster Loop, 1901
Above, the Loop the Loop in Atlantic City featured a twin loop. The umbrellas were out to block the sunlight. Several umbrellas advertised the Lit Brothers, who "trimmed" hats free of charge—perhaps an adjustment needed after riding the coaster in a skimmer or bowler. Library of Congress

Thompson Scenic Railway Company was formed to develop scenic railways throughout America. At the same time, others took out patents on their versions of scenic railways. Building them taller, longer, and faster, each was designed for more thrills than the competition.

It was not long before someone decided it was time to flip upside down on a roller coaster. The French experimented with this idea in 1848 when the first looping coast-

16

er opened at the Frascati Gardens. More of spectacle than a ride, the loop stood 30 feet high and had a long straight run that was needed in order to gain momentum to complete the loop. The strain was too much on the passengers, however, so the coaster was deemed unfeasible.

A similar lesson was learned in 1900 when Lina Beecher took the first step in turning American coaster riders upside down on his loop ride, called the Flip-Flap. Located at Coney Island, this ride took less than 10 seconds, as a small car carrying two passengers coasted down an incline, picking up enough speed to complete the loop. Entering into the 30-foot-high perfect loop, it is said that a person would feel the equivalent force of 12 G's. The ride stirred interest but gave riders neck pains as the cars went through the

Loop the Loop, circa 1903
Above, the Loop the Loop opened at Luna Park, Coney Island, in 1903. Roller coaster loops always attracted observers who would stare in the air, oblivious to the goings-on around them while the car was defying gravity—notice the warning to observers, "Beware of pickpockets."
Library of Congress

17

loop. Before it was dismantled, people would pay to just watch the ride operate.

Although these first attempts at a looping coaster were far from perfect, they did encourage another inventor to try his hand. In 1901, Edward Prescott hired engineer E. A. Green to help him redesign the looping coaster. To lower the G-forces developed during the ride, they created a loop that was an oval rather than a true circle. Loop-the-Loop, as it was called, opened in Atlantic City as an engineering victory. Although this ride was the focus of much attention, it did not become a financial success due to its low rider turnover rate of four riders every 5 minutes. Turning coasters upside down would have to wait until the introduction of steel tracks in the early 1970s.

Figure-Eight, 1905
Below, the Figure-Eight in Nantasket Beach, Massachusetts, featured the thrill of a coaster track criss-crossing above itself.
Library of Congress

The first true standard roller coaster to appear at amusement parks during the turn of the century was the Figure-Eight. As the name hinted, the ride followed a track that wove over and under itself.

Like the scenic railway, the Figure-Eight was a side-friction coaster, referring to the friction wheels that were mounted on the side of the cars. Yet unlike the scenic railways, there was no building with scenic paintings to pass through.

At the time, the Figure-Eight was considered a wild, exciting ride. One such coaster designed by Fred Ingersoll and located at Kennywood Park in Pennsylvania between 1901 and 1921 was described by a writer for the *Pittsburgh Bulletin*: "You were hauled up an incline in a gaudy

Figure-Eight, 1907
Below, due to its popularity, the Figure-Eight layout could be found almost everywhere. This coaster was built in Coffeyville, Kansas.
Library of Congress

COPYRIGHT. 1907.
BY W. E McKINNEY. COFFEYVILLE. KANS.

little car and then let loose, down, under, over, through, up and around and back to the starting place at such a speed and by so many turnings and doublings that you lost all sense of direction and all coherence of ideas."

The fad of the Figure-Eight was short-lived, however, due to new innovations. By the 1920s, most of the original Figure-Eight had either been torn down or expanded and developed into more action-packed rides.

In 1909, John Miller introduced America to the racing

coaster—and with it, the final significant piece of engineering in this era of coaster design. The racing coaster featured two cars run side by side down mirror-image courses; the first car to the bottom won the "race."

But it was an engineering innovation created by Miller with the racing coaster that revolutionized the ride. Miller attached a third set of wheels to the car *under* the track. Until now, the train relied on one set of wheels on top of the track and another set on the inside to create the side friction. This

Flooded Coaster, 1913
Above, perhaps this was the source of the water plume ride? This coaster in the small community of Vandalia, Illinois, was flooded out by the Kaskaskia River. Many small towns built wooden roller coasters during this early wave of coasters' popularity.
Library of Congress

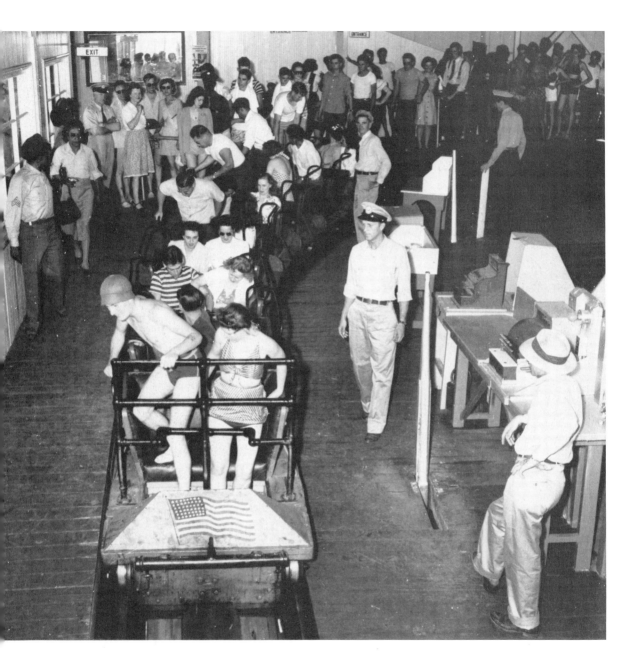

Giant Dipper, 1958
Above, the Giant Dipper at Santa Cruz, California, was a typical coaster of the 1950s with webbing seatbelts and pipe rail restraints for safety. Santa Cruz Beach Boardwalk

third set ensured safety by preventing the coaster trains from jumping the track while gliding over hills. Miller's third-wheel design is still the standard to this day.

*T*he 1920s was the dawn of the Golden Age of roller coasters. World War I had ended and the economy was booming, resulting in a carefree America. The Roar-

MOUNTAIN SPEEDWAY
One Mile of Spine-Tingling Thrills!
On the Beach — Galveston, Texas

ing Twenties was a time of daredevilish challenge, and the coasters built during this decade reflect this attitude. New designs flourished with tracks twisting and turning in and out of dark tunnels and down first drops from a 100-foot-high lift. Names such as Cyclone, Blue Streak, Flying Turns, and Whirlwind were indicative of the new breed of coasters.

The number of coasters grew following the turn of the century to reach a peak of about 1,500 by 1929. Along with the growth of suburbs and an increasing number of automobiles, amusement parks appeared throughout the United States. Trolley lines were no longer the primary source of transportation, and parks became more accessible. In order to get people to drive to their park, each park owner would try to build the highest, fastest, and most terrifying coaster, beginning an era of roller coaster wars.

One Mile of Spine-Tingling Thrills, 1935
Above, the Golden Age of roller coasters spread the thrills all across America and giant wooden coasters such as the Mountain Speedway on the beach in Galveston, Texas, were built to satisfy our craving for scares. The Mountain Speedway was later demolished. Curt Teich Postcard Archives, Lake County, Illinois, Museum

Coney Island, circa 1920s
Right, the fabulous Coney Island was the home of several roller coasters. This was one of the entrances to the park, with a coaster running overhead.
Library of Congress

Famous Roller Coaster Designers

The annals of roller coaster lore are highlighted by many famous designers who tried their hands at creating coasters that could deliver the most thrills and chills.

Philadelphia Toboggan Company has long been one of the leading coaster designers. The firm, working with designers such as **Herbert Schmeck** and **John Allen**, crafted such coasters as The Wildcat (1927) at Lake Compounce Festival Park in Bristol, Connecticut, a classic example of the Golden Age of coaster architecture. The company also created the Giant (1917) at Paragon Park (moved to Wild World in Mitchellville, Maryland, and renamed Wild One); Flying Comet (1940) at Whalom Park in Fitchburg, Massachusetts; The Great American Scream Machine (1973) at Six Flags Over Georgia in Atlanta; and numerous others.

Frank Prior and **Frederick Church** were a renowned coaster design team that created many classic coasters. Giant Dipper (1925) at Belmont Park in San Diego, California, was one of their masterpieces.

Arthur Looff was one of the Golden Age coaster designers, famous for building the Giant Dipper at Santa Cruz Beach Boardwalk in Santa Cruz, California. Looff envisioned a giant wooden roller coaster that would be a "combination of earthquake, balloon ascension, and aeroplane drop." In 1987, the Giant Dipper was honored as a National Historic Landmark.

E. Joy Morris designed Leap-the-Dips (1902) at Lakemont Park in Altoona, Pennsylvania, the world's oldest coaster still operating and the only remaining "side friction figure-eight," which was a popular design style from about 1900 to 1920.

Ed Vettel designed the famous Blue Streak (1937) at Conneaut Lake Park, Pennsylvania, which is noted for its unique "camel humps"—a series of three dramatic hills that occur in breathtakingly quick succession on the "out" side of the ride's 2900-foot-long circuit. Ed Vettel's nephew, **Andy Vettel**, has continued the family tradition, designing coasters such as Thunderbolt (1968) at Kennywood in West Mifflin, Pennsylvania.

National Amusement Device Company of Dayton, Ohio, built Zippin Pippin (1915) at Libertyland in Memphis, Tennessee, which is one of the oldest operating wooden roller coasters in North America and is said to have been a favorite of Elvis Presley.

Miller and Baker was one of America's top coaster firms, creating such coasters as Jack Rabbit (1922) at Kennywood in West Mifflin, Pennsylvania, which was designed by John A. Miller.

Arrow Dynamics was at the forefront of the revival in roller coaster popularity. Arrow has created many of the quintessential coaster designs currently thrilling riders from Disneyland to Dollywood. Arrow conceived the runaway mine train-style of coaster, such as Cedar Creek Mine Ride (1969) at Cedar Point in Sandusky, Ohio. Arrow also designed the magnificent $8 million Magnum XL-200 (1989) at Cedar Point, which was listed in the *1990 Guinness Book of World Records* as the world's fastest coaster with the longest drop.

Bolliger & Mabillard of Switzerland have designed numerous coasters, including Raptor (1994) at Cedar Point in Sandusky, Ohio, the world's tallest, longest, and fastest of its kind. Among the firm's most exciting coasters is Vortex (1992) at Paramount's Carowinds, which designer Claude Mabillard declared "the best coaster Bolliger & Mabillard has built up to now."

Anton Schwarzkopf of Germany designed many US theme park coasters. hIs Revolution (1976) at Six Flags Magic Mountain in Valencia, California, was the world's first giant looping roller coaster with G-forces of 4.94 when entering the loop.

Curtis D. Summers designed Mean Streak (1991) at Cedar Point in Sandusky, Ohio, the world's second tallest wooden coaster. Mean Streak was constructed by the **Charles Dinn Corporation**.

National Amusement Devices created many coasters for American theme parks, the last being the woodie Wildcat (1968) now at Frontier City in Oklahoma City, Oklahoma.

Custom Coaster, Inc., created The Sky Princess (1992) at Dutch Wonderland in Lancaster, Pennsylvania, a 2000-foot-long wooden out-and-back.

International Coaster, Inc., created, among other coasters, The Hurler (1994), a massive 3157-foot-long woodie at Paramount's Carowinds and King's Dominion.

Roger Tofte and **Dave Windows** created Ice Mountain Bobsled (1982) at Enchanted Forest in Turner, Oregon, an original design with a 2000-foot-long steel track undulating down a mountainside including two lifts.

O. D. Hopkins Associates, Inc., created the Texas Tornado (1985) at Wonderland Park in Amarillo, Texas, which includes a 200-foot-long tunnel 13 feet under the ground.

John Pierce & Associates designed Rattler (1992) at Fiesta Texas in San Antonio, Texas. Built by the **Roller Coaster Corporation of Texas**, this mammoth coaster is built around a limestone quarry and includes tunnels within the quarry walls. It opened with four world records: the tallest wooden coaster; longest first drop of any woodie; fastest woodie; and the steepest first drop of a wooden coaster.

William Cobb created numerous coasters, the last of which was the Tree Topper (1989) at Upper Clements Park in Clementsport, Nova Scotia, Canada.

Vekoma International of The Netherlands has designed numerous coasters for US theme parks, including Boomerang (1990) at Knotts Berry Farm in Buena Park, California. Boomerang turns riders upside down six times in less than 1 minute. Vekoma International has created many novel coasters, including Chaos (1989) at Opryland in Nashville, Tennessee, which is the first of its kind in the world. Completely enclosed, Chaos combines traditional roller coaster thrills with state-of-the-art audio and visual technology to give a sense of motion, sight, sound, and touch.

In 1927, the highest wooden coaster of the time was built in Poughkeepsie, New York: The Blue Streak was a 138-foot-high legend of the day. The Blue Streak battled the famous Cyclone, which is today the most popular remnant of the Golden Age.

Located at Coney Island's Astroland, the 1927 Cyclone is proof that quality survives. Even today it is the benchmark by which other coasters are judged. Designed by Vernon Keenan and Harry Baker, the Cyclone careens down an amazingly sharp 60-degree first drop, taking riders on an 85-foot plunge. Its earliest top speed has been lost to history, but today's Cyclone, with the help of bimetal rails and computers, *averages* 60 miles per hour. The trip along the rickety-sounding course takes just 1 minute and 40 seconds as passengers navigate its eight steep hills and valleys. As famed coaster designer John Allen said, "Part of

Out-and-Back Design
Right, the Great American Scream Machine at Six Flags Over Georgia is one of the best examples of the out-and-back roller coaster design.

Runaway Mine Train
Above, the runaway mine train-type of coaster ride was created by the prolific Arrow Dynamics company in the 1960s and this coaster style soon spread throughout American amusement parks. This Runaway Mine Train was the first at Six Flags Over Texas, built in 1966.

the appeal is the imagined danger."

The Cyclone's imagined danger—along with the fact that the Cyclone paid off its $175,000 cost within the first year of its use—inspired many a roller coaster designer and park owner. Among these was Harry Traver. Notorious for many wicked coasters in the 1920s (all of which are now extinct), the name Traver became synonymous with Cyclone.

The scariest of the Traver creations were the Cyclones at Crystal Beach Park in Ontario, Canada; at Palisades Park in New Jersey; and the Lightning at Revere Beach, Massachusetts. Although regarded as wooden coasters, they were actually steel structures with a layered wood track. They were enjoyed not only due to their height—they were 96 feet tall—but for what they did to one's body. They were fast, breathtaking, and rough; the Cyclone in Crystal Beach had a registered nurse on duty at all times. Although it only existed from 1928 to 1947, this coaster is still considered the most vicious ride ever.

Also built in 1928 was the Aeroplane coaster at Playland Amusement Park in Rye Beach, New York. For this coaster, Traver teamed up with Frederick Church. The Aeroplane boasted an 85-foot lift hill that dropped into a spiral track banked so steeply that riders were slammed against the sides of the cars. The cars themselves tilted so far over that it appeared they would crash. This coaster was torn down in 1957, but was considered the masterpiece of the Golden Age.

During this era, the roller coaster lived through many transformations. The Golden Age was capped with the opening of the Bobs at Manchester, England, in 1929. This coaster took riders on an adventure that reached a maximum speed of 61 miles per hour. While this was the fastest coaster of the time, the Cyclone at Crystal Beach ranked as "the most fearsome," and the Bobs at Chicago's Riverview Park and the Aeroplane at Rye Beach were considered "the most beautiful."

Like so many other businesses, the roller coaster fell victim to the national economic woes of the Great Depression. The furious building pace of the twenties screeched to a sudden halt. Park attendance was down. Owners could not afford to maintain coasters or pay for insurance. Hundreds of coasters were abandoned or torn down and few new ones were built during the next forty years. Furthermore, World War II brought with it wood and rubber rationing,

Front or Back Seat: The Great Debate

On a roller coaster, the choice of seat will determine your ride. Some prefer the front for a smoother sensation and the feeling of being alone. Others insist that the best seat is in the last car of the train. The last seat acts like the tail end of a whip as it slams from side to side and pulls you swiftly over the tops of hills.

Regardless of seating preference, it is generally accepted that the best time to ride is at night. The roller coaster is a great attraction because it can be a different ride at different times.

leading to the decline of old suburban amusement parks. From a Golden Age peak of around 1,500 rides, the coaster population dwindled to less than 200 by 1960.

By the mid-1950s, a revival of the roller coasters and theme parks was taking place in the United States. Since the Golden Age in the Roaring Twenties, the times had changed on all fronts—politically, economically, and socially.

Television had been introduced and almost immediately captured America's leisure time. The aging amusement parks of the past were now in direct competition with this new form of entertainment. When Walt Disney decided to create a park, however, he used this new medium to his advantage by promoting his new theme park with a show called "Disneyland." This successful marketing ploy led to the opening of Disneyland in Anaheim, California, on July 17, 1955.

Not too far from Disneyland, America's first "theme" park was still in operation—and had been since 1940. Old West Ghost Town was created by Walter Knott near his berry stand and was the first park to orient itself completely around a particular theme. As the years went on, more theme sections were added, and today it is the country's most popular independently owned theme park.

Knott's modest beginning was helped considerably by the overwhelming success of Disneyland. Disneyland was the first planned theme park and its opening marked the birth of the modern amusement park. As parks sprung up throughout the United States in Disneyland's wake, it became apparent that the revival of the roller coaster would soon follow.

The modern park differs from the old amusement park in that it typically revolves around a theme, and by enclosing several attractions within a park's borders and using the pay-one-price concept, showmen were able to monopolize a customer's time—and money.

The roots of the modern amusement park lies in the old amusement park with the only difference being that modern parks tend to revolve around a theme.

Traditional parks were first developed at Coney Island. Sea Lion Park, which later changed its name to Luna Park, was the first to open at Coney Island, in 1895. Dreamland and Steeplechase Park soon followed as showmen found they could monopolize a customer's time—and money—by enclosing several attractions within a park's borders and using the pay-one-price concept. Before this time, each ride had been individually owned.

This park idea caught on and spread like wildfire throughout the East Coast. Whalom Park was established in the late 1800s and has survived over the years. Situated on the picturesque shores of Lake Whalom in Lunenburg, Massachusetts, this amusement park is one of the oldest. Many amusement parks at the time were purchased by the local street railroad company; Whalom Park was bought by the Fitchburg and Leominster Street Railway Company in 1892. Local street railway companies were charged a flat rate for their power, but since this rate did not always relate to the number of riders, owners developed the parks at the end of the railway line in order to sell fares during slow periods—weeknights and weekends—to help offset the cost of power. The idea was so popular that virtually every area had one or more street railway parks.

The next step toward modern theme parks was Playland Park in Rye Beach, New York. In the mid-1920s, the Westchester County Park Commission purchased part of Rye Beach with the idea of creating a completely planned park suitable for families, much like Disney's goal in the 1950s. The commission's intent was to create an "unequaled seaside public park to provide clean, wholesome recreation for people of Westchester County."

After studying other amusement parks of the day, Playland became America's first totally planned amusement park and the prototype for today's theme parks. Frank W. Darling was hired to oversee the construction and become the first manager of the park. His credentials included former manager of a Coney Island park, President of the L. A. Thompson Scenic Railway Company and President of the National Association of Amusement Parks. It was his association with Fred Church (Traver/Church) that brought the famous Aeroplane coaster to Playland.

With the overwhelming success of Disneyland after its opening in the 1950s, the planned theme park became the wave of the future and the springboard of the coaster revival. While Disneyland was prominent in reviving the roller coaster, Six Flags is perhaps more responsible for leading the revival.

Beginning in 1961, Six Flags' original park was located exactly midway between Dallas and Fort Worth, Texas, on the former Waggoner DDD Ranch. The idea was to draw the bulk of its guests from within a 300-mile radius, and like Disneyland, Six Flags based its operation on a wholesome atmosphere and grounds that were kept immaculately clean at all times. This regional theme park led to others around the country, which today are home to some of the world's greatest roller coasters.

Most modern parks contain an updated version of the famous Coney Island Scenic Railway, using tubular steel tracks instead of a wooden track. These rides were the brainchildren of Arrow Dynamics and usually took the theme of runaway mine trains. These new coasters were actually cousins to the first steel tubular tracked Matterhorn roller coaster at Disneyland.

Arrow Dynamics was a small machine shop in northern California when it was commissioned in 1946 to build a carousel for the San Jose City Park. Arrow's work caught the eye of Walt Disney, who was impressed with the quality and craftsmanship and realized that he had found a source to help make his dream of Disneyland a reality. He bought one-third of the business that would eventually design and build an entire series of unique rides for his park, including Snow White, Peter Pan, Dumbo, The Mad Hatter's Tea Party, and the Casey Jr. Circus Train.

In 1959, Arrow took its first venture into roller coasters by manufacturing Disney's Matterhorn Bobsled ride. A true innovation in engineering and construction, the Matterhorn became the first modern all-steel coaster, using a tubular track and nylon wheels on the trains. This ride became the basis for a new breed of coasters and its success created a tremendous demand on Arrow by the new parks for similar rides; one of the next Arrow creations was the runaway mine train coasters. Steel coasters became popular because they resulted in a smooth, more silent, ride. They also enabled designers to build spirals and turns not feasible with wooden tracks. Steel coaster construction would flourish during the next few years.

Steel coasters became popular because they resulted in a smooth, silent ride and enabled designers to build spirals and turns not feasible with wooden tracks.

Racing Coaster, 1918
Above, racing coasters featured two side-by-side tracks and the cars raced around the circuit. The Jack Rabbit Racer was built on a pier at Long Beach, California, in 1900. It was later demolished. Curt Teich Postcard Archives, Lake County, Illinois, Museum

*I*n 1972, a wooden twin-track coaster called the Racer opened at Kings Island just outside of Cincinnati, Ohio. Designed by John Allen, this wooden coaster played a prominent role in reviving the interest in wooden roller coasters in the United States.

John Allen created five wooden roller coasters between 1972 and 1976, each bigger and better than its predecessor. All were basically out-and-backs, a speedy design that follows a relatively straight, but undulated, path out from the station into a banked curve, and then returns back along a course roughly parallel to the first. Allen, who was associated with the Philadelphia Toboggan Company, used this pattern to emphasize speed and quick gravity shifts.

Since the opening of the Racer, dozens of new wooden coasters have been built, each attempting to outdo the other in height, length, and speed. This new surge has much to do with the advances made in engineering and technology.

*T*he basic principle of a roller coaster remains the same today: The train is released at the ride's highest point so as to maximize the amount of gravitational potential energy. It is this potential energy that allows the train enough momentum to coast over the entire track or until it encounters another lift hill. No hill can be higher than the initial lift since it would require more energy than the train began with. The speed is also determined by the height and slope of the first hill. Assuming a drop at a 55-degree angle, the lift hill would have to be 400 feet tall to give the train a speed of 100 miles per hour. Velocity equals the square root of two times gravity times height.

Other considerations must be addressed including wind drag and the friction between the wheels and the track. These energy losses—along with gravity—must be balanced so that the train will not stop anywhere on the track other than at the loading station.

Another important consideration in designing a coaster is related to the forces it will unleash. Known as G-force or "G's," this is the pressure felt by riders as they reach the bottom of a hill and begin to climb again. On the other

Ride Centerline Layout
Below, this designer's overhead view of the Iron Dragon coaster, built by Arrow Dynamics at Cedar Point in Sandusky, Ohio, in 1987, shows the care that goes into building thrills. Each corner is analyzed for the center of the curve, curve radius, arc, and arc length.
Arrow Dynamics

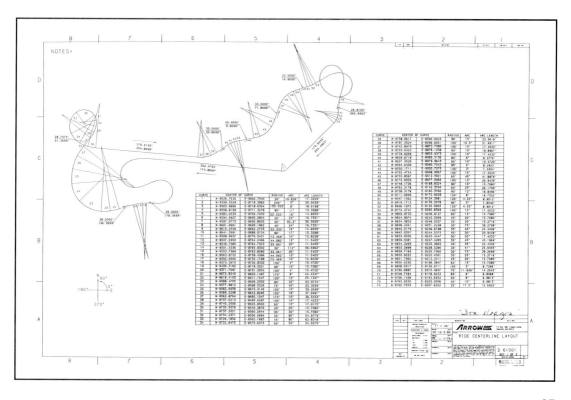

Coaster Brake

Right, the modern roller coaster uses a brake unit that operates much like a disc brake on an automobile. A fin is attached to the underside of the coaster cars; as the fin enters the brake unit, air pressure is released, closing the brake pads, squeezing the fin, and bringing the train to a smooth, safe stop. Philadelphia Toboggan Company

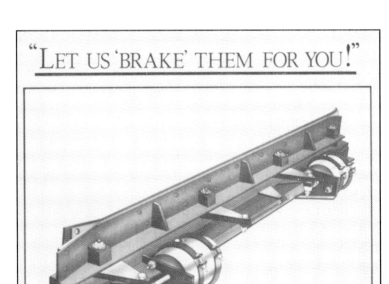

hand, riders feel the sensation of floating or negative G-force when the train flies over a hill.

Another force felt may be due to the curves on a track. As the train turns along a curve, there is a sideways force felt if the track has not been banked to the optimum angle. This is generally the case because of space restrictions, which call for turns to be made without the perfect angle. Many coasters are designed this way, however, in order to give a rougher ride.

Gone are the days of trial and error. Today, roller coaster design is a science, and designers are precise, relying on computers to help calculate the coaster's exact dimensions. Engineers feed all information into the computer to measure all potential forces upon a rider. At the turn of the century, little was known about gravity forces and the effect they had on passengers. Today, engineering and computer skills are essential in the design process; physicians are often consulted about the biomechanics of a ride. To get a simplistic, hands on example of this, visitors at Walt Disney World's EPCOT Center can play with a coaster computer. Located in Communicore East, this computer allows you to lay out a roller coaster track and then simulates the ride.

With new technology and the introduction of steel track in the Matterhorn and the runaway mine trains, designers were able to create smooth, twisting courses that were mild versions of the larger wooden coasters. Many coaster buffs claimed that the smoother ride took away the excitement, however. To many, it seemed that technology was taking a step backward.

*D*esigners then discovered that steel could be used to turn the cars upside down. The main breakthrough was the development of the corkscrew by Arrow in 1975, offering riders head-over-heels excitement as a substitute for smoothing out the sometimes bruising rides of the woodies. The steel track is made of round pipe so that the train's three sets of wheels can be contoured to fit and keep the train from falling in the unlikely event that it stops while upside down.

Coaster builders had been trying to perfect a loop since the late 1800s, but Arrow finally found the correct configuration. By changing the shape of the loop into an elliptical corkscrew, Arrow found that the G-force could be reduced to a comfortable level. The force on the earlier circle loops was around 12 G's—Air Force fighter pilots can only tolerate 11 G's before blacking out! Still, when Arrow built a full-scale prototype of the corkscrew, it found a heavy G-load, but the designers' concerns were lessened when they found similar forces on the Giant Dipper, an old wooden coaster in Santa Cruz, California.

The success of the corkscrew was followed by the giant clothoid loop in 1976, a breakthrough that was independently developed by several designers. Teardrop in shape, this loop lowered the centrifugal force placed on riders because it was composed of radii of varying lengths. In a circle loop, the train would require so much speed to com-

Designers soon discovered that steel could be used to turn the coasters upside down. The force on the earlier circle loops was around 12 G's—Air Force fighter pilots can only tolerate 11 G's before blacking out!

Woodies Live On
Above, steel tubular coaster construction has led designers into a brave new world, but that doesn't mean the woodies are gone. Many of the fastest—and most thrilling—coasters are still made of wood. This is the Giant Dipper at Santa Cruz Beach Boardwalk.

plete the rotation that it would place an unbearable force upon riders when entering the loop. The tremendous speed was necessary because the train would decelerate sharply as it reached the top. The teardrop shape, however, smooths out the entry while tightening the top of the loop. This causes an acceleration that helps counteract gravity due to the smaller radius at the top; the shorter the radius, the faster the movement.

The perfection of these loops has led to practically unlimited possibilities. The limits on design today are economics but certainly not physics. When a park is thinking of installing a coaster, the main considerations are maintenance cost and public opinion. The coaster has to pay for itself by bringing people into the park.

Pipeline Prototype
Left, Arrow Dynamics' Pipeline prototype signals the dawn of a new generation of coasters. It should soon be ready for the parks.

In 1989, attendance at the nation's amusement and theme parks rose a projected 1.6 percent. Seven parks that added new coasters, however, enjoyed an average attendance boost of 8.5 percent. At that rate, roller coasters will repay the investment within two years of operation.

What does the future hold? The seventies brought back the woodie, but the steel track dominated the coaster boom. As it evolved, steel tracks took us through corkscrews, vertical loops, and boomerangs. It took us upside down while sitting and standing—and even suspended us below the track. Now Arrow is working on a concept that will simulate snap rolls like that of an airplane. Called the Pipeline, this design will have the train running between the tubular track giving it greater flexibility to rotate as it speeds along its course.

The future looks bright for roller coasters of all types.

Vertical Loop
Left, the vertical loop of White Lightnin' at Carowinds. White Lightnin' has since been closed and sold, hopefully to open at another park soon.

Upside-Down Coaster
Opposite page, Arrow Dynamics' first upside-down roller coaster, the Corkscrew at Knotts Berry Farm, features two 360 degree loops through which passengers are carried at speeds of up to 45 miles per hour. This coaster is now located at Silverwood Theme Park in Coeur D'Alene, Idaho.

Five Years of Fright
Left, in 1989, the famed Big Bad Wolf roller coaster at Busch Gardens, The Old Country in Williamsburg, Virginia, celebrated five years of transporting visitors at the speed of fright. The uniquely suspended coaster whips through Bavarian villages before plunging 80 feet to the Rhine River below.

Dawn of a New Era
Right, today's coaster are bigger, faster, and safer. The Magnum XL-200 at Cedar Point has a lift hill of 205 feet and reaches 72 miles per hour on the first drop.

Nessie at Night
Opposite page, the action of the famed Loch Ness Monster, one of the largest coasters in the world, continues at night at Busch Gardens, The Old Country in Williamsburg, Virginia. The European-themed park is open evenings throughout the summer season.

Stand-Up Coaster
Right, Kings Dominion's stand-up roller coaster, Shockwave, features a 95-foot drop, a 360-degree loop, and a 540-degree helix through which the track is banked 80 degrees, making riders feel as if they are standing parallel to the ground.

Stand-Up Coaster
Above, King Cobra was the first roller coaster of its kind in America designed to carry riders in a standing position. It opened at Kings Island in April 1984. The $3 million steel coaster features a 360-degree vertical loop and a horizontal loop.

Chronology of Wooden Coasters
Still in Operation

Year Built	Roller Coaster
1902	Leap-the-Dips, Lakemont Park, Altoona, PA
1915	Zippin Pippin, Libertyland, Memphis, TN
1917	The Wild One, Wild World, Mitchellville, MD (opened 1986)
1919	Jack Rabbit, Clementon Lake, Clementon, NJ
1920	Jack Rabbit, Seabreeze, Rochester, NY
1921	Jack Rabbit, Kennywood, West Mifflin, PA
1921	The Roller Coaster, Lagoon, Farmington, UT
1923	Thunderhawk, Dorney Park, Allentown, PA
1924	Thunderbolt, Kennywood, West Mifflin, PA
1924	Giant Dipper, Santa Cruz Beach Boardwalk, Santa Cruz, CA
1925	Giant Dipper, Belmont Park, San Diego, CA
1926	The Big Dipper, Geauga Lake, Aurora, OH
1927	Screachin' Eagle, Americana, Middletown, OH
1927	Giant Coaster, Arnold's Park, Arnold's Park, IA
1927	Cyclone, Astroland, Coney Island, NY
1927	The Racer, Kennywood, West Mifflin, PA
1927	The Wildcat, Lake Compounce Festival Park, Bristol, CT
1929	Dragon Coaster, Playland Park, Rye, NY
1929	Wild Cat, Electric Park (proposed), from Idora Park, Indianapolis, IN
1929	Cyclone, Williams Grove, Williams Grove, PA
1930	The Yankee Cannonball, Canobie Lake Park, Salem, NH
1935	Roller Coaster, The Puyallup Fair, Puyallup, WA
1936	The Wildcat, Elitch Gardens, Denver, CO
1937	Blue Streak, Conneaut Lake Park, Conneaut Lake Park, PA
1938	Rollo Coaster, Idlewild, Ligonier, PA
1940	Flyer Comet, Whalom Park, Fitchburg, MA
1940	Cyclone Coaster, Lakeside, Denver, CO
1941	Thunderbolt, Riverside, Agawam, MA
1947	Comet, The Great Escape, Lake George, NY (from Crystal Beach)
1947	Phoenix, Knoebel's Amusement Resort, Elysburg, PA (reopened in 1985)
1949	Roller Coaster, Joyland, Wichita, KS
1951	Comet, Waldameer, Erie, PA
1958	Big Dipper, Camden Park, Huntington, WV
1959	Coaster, Playland, Vancouver, BC
1960	Skyliner, Lakemont Park, Altoona, PA
1963	Starliner, Miracle Strip, Panama City, FL
1964	The Blue Streak, Cedar Point, Sandusky, OH
1965	The Twister, Elitch Gardens, Denver, CO
1966	Swamp Fox, Family Kingdom, Myrtle Beach, SC
1967	Cannonball, Lake Winnepesaukan, Rossville, GA
1968	Wildcat, Frontier City, Oklahoma City, OK
1968	Zingo, Bell's Amusement Park, Tulsa, OK
1972	The Racer, Paramounts Kings Island, Cincinnati, OH

1973	The Great American Scream Machine, Six Flags Over Georgia, Atlanta, GA
1974	Rebel Yell, Paramounts Kings Dominion, Doswell, VA
1975	High Roller, Valleyfair, Shakopee, MN
1976	Screamin' Eagle, Six Flags Over Mid-America, Eureka, MO
1976	Texas Cyclone, Astroworld, Houston, TX
1976	Thunder Road, Paramounts Carowinds, Charlotte, NC
1978	Arkansas Twister, Magic Springs, Hot Springs, AR
	(from Boardwalk and Baseball in Florida, "Hurricane")
1978	Colossus, Six Flags Magic Mountain, Valencia, CA
1978	Tornado, Adventureland, Des Moines, IA
1979	The Beast, Paramounts Kings Island, Cincinnati, OH
1979	Rolling Thunder, Six Flags Great Adventure, Jackson, NJ
1981	Mighty Canadian Minebuster, Canada's Wonderland, Maple, ONT
1980	Judge Roy Scream, Six Flags Over Texas, Arlington, TX
1981	Wilde Beast, Canada's Wonderland, Maple, ONT
1981	American Eagle, Six Flags Great America, Gurnee, IL
1982	The Grizzly, Paramounts Kings Dominion, Doswell, VA
1983	The Riverside Cyclone, Riverside Amusement Park, Agawam, MA
1985	Le Monstre, La Ronde, Montreal, QUE
1986	The Grizzly, Paramounts Great America, Santa Clara, CA
1988	The Raging Wolf Bobs, Geauga Lake, Aurora, OH
1988	Wolverine Wildcat, Michigan's Adventure, Muskegan, MI
1989	Timber Wolf, Worlds of Fun, Kansas City, MO
1989	Hercules, Dorney Park, Allentown, PA
1989	Tree Topper, Upper Clements Theme Park, Clementsport, NS
1990	Predator, Darien Lake, Darien Center, NY
1990	Georgia Cyclone, Six Flags Over Georgia, Atlanta, GA
1990	Thunder Run, Kentucky Kingdom, Louisville, KY
1990	Texas Giant, Six Flags Over Texas, Arlington, TX
1991	Psyclone, Six Flags Magic Mountain, Valencia, CA
1991	The Mean Streak, Cedar Point, Sandusky, OH
1992	Sky Princess, Dutch Wonderland, Lancaster, PA
1992	Rattler, Fiesta Texas, San Antonio, TX
1993	The Outlaw, Adventureland, Des Moines, IA
1993	Toronado, Stricker's Grove, Hamilton, OH
1994	The Hoosier Hurricane, Indiana Beach, Monticello, IN
1994	The Hurler, Paramount's Kings Dominion, Doswell, VA
1994	The Hurler, Paramount's Carowinds, Charlotte, NC

Chronology of Steel Coasters
Still in Operation

Year Built	Roller Coaster
1959	Matterhorn, Disneyland, Anaheim, CA
1960	Golden Nugget Mine Train, Conko's Party Pier, Wildwood, NJ
1966	Runaway Mine Train, Six Flags Over Texas, Arlington, TX
1967	Dahlonega Mine Train, Six Flags Over Georgia, Atlanta, GA
1969	Cedar Creek Mine Ride, Cedar Point, Sandusky, OH
1971	River King Mine Train, Six Flags Over Mid-America, Eureka, MO
1971	Thunder Express, Dollywood, Pigeon Forge, TN (moved here in 1989)
1971	Gold Rusher, Six Flags Magic Mountain, Valencia, CA
1972	Goldrusher, Paramounts Carowinds, Charlotte, NC
1972	Excalibur, Astroworld, Houston, TX
1972	Rock'n'Roller Coaster, Opryland, Nashville, TN
1972	Jumbo Jet, Glenball Ltd., Brooklyn, NY
1973	Runaway Train, Six Flags Great Adventure, Jackson, NJ
1973	Zambezi Zinger, Worlds of Fun, Kansas City, MO
1974	Sky Streek, Boblo Island, Detroit, MI
1974	Trail Blazer Coaster, Hersheypark, Hershey, PA
1974	Jet Star II, Lagoon, Farmington, UT (relocated 1976)
1975	Corkscrew, Silverwood Park, Coeur D'alene, ID (moved here in 1990)
1975	Canobie Corkscrew, Canobie Lake Park, Salem, NH (moved here in 1990)
1975	Space Mountain, Walt Disney World, Lake Buena Vista, FL
1975	Wabash Cannonball, Opryland, Nashville, TN
1976	Python, Busch Gardens: The Dark Continent, Tampa, FL
1976	City Jet, Wonderland Pier, Ocean City, NJ
1976	Corkscrew, Cedar Point, Sandusky, OH
1976	The Whizzer, Six Flags Great America, Gurnee, IL
1976	The Demon, Six Flags Great America, Gurnee, IL
1976	Wacky Soap Box Racers, Knott's Berry Farm, Buena Park, CA
1976	The Whizzer, Paramounts Great America, Santa Clara, CA
1976	Revolution, Six Flags Magic Mountain, Valencia, CA
1977	Space Mountain, Disneyland, Anaheim, CA
1977	The Tidal Wave, Paramounts Great America, Santa Clara, CA
1977	Double Loop, Geauga Lake, Aurora, OH
1977	Afterburner, Fun Spot Park, Angola, IN (relocated 1991)
1977	Sooperdooperlooper, Hersheypark, Hershey, PA
1977	Jet Star, Morey's Pier, Wildwood, NJ (moved here from Knoebels)
1977	Black Widow, Riverside, Agawam, MA
1977	Thunderbolt Express, Camden Park, Huntington, WV
1977	Nightmare Mine, Frontier City, Oklahoma City, OK
1978	Greezed Lightnin', Astroworld, Houston, TX
1978	Corkscrew, Myrtle Beach Pavilion, Myrtle Beach, SC
1978	Shock Wave, Six Flags Over Texas, Arlington, TX
1978	Mind Bender, Six Flags Over Georgia, Atlanta, GA
1978	The Loch Ness Monster, Busch Gardens: The Old Country, Williamsburg, VA

1978	Comet, Hersheypark, Hershey, PA (wooden structure:1946)
1978	Steamin' Demon, The Great Escape, Lake George, NY (relocated here in 1984)
1978	Lightnin' Loops, Six Flags Great Adventure, Jackson, NJ
1978	Gemini, Cedar Point, Sandusky, OH (wooden structure)
1978	Corkscrew, Geauga Lake, Aurora, OH
1978	Tidal Wave, Six Flags Great America, Gurnee, IL
1978	Montezooma's Revenge, Knott's Berry Farm, Buena Park, CA
1979	Big Thunder Mountain Railroad, Disneyland, Anaheim, CA
1979	Wild Rails, Valleyfair, Shakopee, MN
1979	Corkscrew, Michigan's Adventure, Muskegon, MI
1979	Silver Bullet, Frontier City, Oklahoma City, OK (moved here in 1986)
1979	Revolution, Libertyland, Memphis, TN
1980	Sidewinder, Elitch Gardens, Denver, CO (relocated 1990)
1980	The Demon, Paramounts Great America, Santa Clara, CA
1980	Carolina Cyclone, Paramounts Carowinds, Charlotte, NC
1980	Big Thunder Mountain Railroad, Walt Disney World, Lake Vuena Vista, FL
1980	Corkscrew, Valleyfair, Shakopee, MN
1980	Orient Express, Worlds of Fun, Kansas City, MO
1981	Time Twister, Jolly Roger, Ocean City, MD (moved here in 1987)
1981	Dragon Fyre, Canada's Wonderland, Maple, ONT
1981	Le Super Manege, La Ronde, Montreal, QUE
1981	Scorpion, Busch Gardens: The Dark Continent, Tampa, FL
1981	Viper, Astroworld, Houston, TX (relocated here in 1989)
1982	Ice Mountain Bobsled, Enchanted Forest, Turner, OR
1982	Fire Dragon, Lagoon, Farmington, UT (relocated 1983)
1982	Turn of the Century, Calaway Park, Calgary, ALB
1982	The Viper, Darien Lake, Darien Center, NY
1983	Dragon Mountain, Marineland, Niagara Falls, ONT
1984	Whirlwind, Knoebels, Elysburg, PA (moved here from Playland)
1984	Sea Serpent, Mariners Landing, Wildwood, NJ
1984	King Cobra, Paramounts Kings Island, Cincinnati, OH
1984	Starchaser, Kentucky Kingdom, Louisville, KY (moved here in 1987)
1984	The Big Bad Wolf, Busch Gardens: The Old Country, Williamsburg, VA
1984	XLR-8, Astroworld, Houston, TX
1985	Texas Toronado, Wonderland Park, Amarillo, TX
1985	The Screamer, Boblo Island, Detroit, MI
1985	Skyrider, Canada's Wonderland, Maple, ONT
1985	Le Boomerang, La Ronde, Montreal, QUE
1985	Loop Corkscrew, Rocky Point, Warwick, RI
1985	Auto Sled, West Edmonton Mall, Edmonton, ALB
1985	Mindbender, West Edmonton Mall, Edmonton, ALB
1986	Flashback, Six Flags Magic Mountain, Valencia, CA (moved here in 1992)
1986	Lazer, Dorney Park, Allentown, PA
1986	Tidal Wave, Trimper's Rides, Ocean City, MD
1986	Ninja, Six Flags Over Mid-America, Eureka, MO (moved here in 1989)
1986	Ultra Twister, Astroworld, Houston, TX (moved here in 1990)
1986	Shockwave, Paramounts Kings Dominion, Doswell, VA

1987	Batman The Escape, Six Flags Astroworld, Houston, TX
	(originally located at Magic Mountain, then Six Flags Great Adventure until 1992)
1987	The Bat, Canada's Wonderland, Maple, ONT
1987	Polar Coaster, Storyland, Glen, NH
1987	Vortex, Paramounts Kings Island, Cincinnati, OH
1987	Iron Dragon, Cedar Point, Sandusky, OH
1988	The Nightmare, Boblo Island, Detroit, MI
1988	Shockwave, Six Flags Great America, Gurnee, IL
1988	Ninja, Six Flags Magic Mountain, Valencia, CA
1988	Red Devil, Ghost Town in the Sky, Maggie Valley, NC
1989	The Ninja, Six Flags Over Georgia, Atlanta, GA (moved here in 1992)
1989	Chaos, Opryland, Nashville, TN
1989	Flashback, Six Flags Over Texas, Arlington, TX
1989	Magnum XL-200, Cedar Point, Sandusky, OH
1989	Excalibur, Valleyfair, Shakopee, MN (wooden structure)
1989	Great American Scream Machine, Six Flags Great Adventure, Jackson, NJ
1990	Iron Wolf, Six Flags Great America, Gurnee, IL
1990	Dragon, Adventureland, Des Moines, IA
1990	Vampire, Kentucky Kingdom, Louisville, KY
1990	Viper, Six Flags Magic Mountain, Valencia, CA
1990	Boomerang, Knott's Berry Farm, Buena Park, CA
1991	Vortex, Paramounts Great America, Santa Clara, CA
1991	Desert Storm, Castles and Coasters, Phoenix, AZ
1991	Patriot, Castles and Coasters, Phoenix, AZ
1991	Anaconda, Paramounts Kings Dominion, Doswell, VA
1991	Adventure Express, Paramounts Kings Island, Cincinnati, OH
1991	Steel Phantom, Kennywood, West Mifflin, PA
1991	Vortex, Canada's Wonderland, Maple, ONT
1991	Hurricane, Long Island Adventureland, East Farmingdale, NY
1992	Sidewinder, Hersheypark, Hershey, PA
1992	Ripsaw, Camp Snoopy, Bloomington, MN
1992	Batman the Ride, Six Flags Great America, Gurnee, IL
1992	Drachen Fire, Busch Gardens: The Old Country, Williamsburg, VA
1992	Vortex, Paramounts Carowinds, Charlotte, NC
1992	Hurricane, Santa Cruz Beach Boardwalk, Santa Cruz, CA
1993	Top Gun, Paramounts Great America, Santa Clara, CA
1993	Canyon Blaster, Grand Slam Canyon, Las Vegas, NV
1993	Gadget's Go Coaster, Disneyland, Anaheim, CA
1993	Kumba, Busch Gardens: The Dark Continent, Tampa, FL
1993	Thunderation, Silver Dollar City, Branson, MO
1993	Top Gun, Paramount's Kings Island, Kings Island, OH
1993	Batman the Ride, Six Flags Great Adventure, Jackson, NJ
1994	Raptor, Cedar Point, Sandusky, OH
1994	Lightning Bolt, MGM Grand, Las Vegas, NV
1994	The Desperado, Buffalo Bill's Wild West Resort, South Stateline, NV
1994	Batman the Ride, Six Flags Magic Mountain, Valencia, CA

1. Upper Clements Park (Clementsport, Nova Scotia, Canada)
2. Canada's Wonderland (Maple Ontario, Canada)
3. La Ronde (Montreal, Quebec, Canada)
4. Marineland (Niagra Falls, Ontario, Canada)
5. Lake Compounce Festival Park (Bristol, Connecticut)
6. Wild World (Mitchellville, Maryland)
7. Riverside Amusement Park (Agawam, Massachusetts)
8. Whalom Park (Fitchburg, Massachusetts)
9. Canoble Lake Park (Salem, New Hampshire)
10. Clemonton Amusement Park (Clementon, New Jersey)
11. Six Flags Great Adventure (Jackson, New Jersey)
12. Astroland (Coney Island, New York)
13. Darien Lake (Darien Center, New York)
14. The Great Escape (Lake George, New York)
15. Seabreeze (Rochester, New York)
16. Playland Park (Rye, New York)
17. Dorney Park (Allentown, Pennsylvania)
18. Lakemont Park (Altoona, Pennsylvania)
19. Conneaut Lake Park (Conneaut Lake Park, Pennsylvania)
20. Knoebels Amusement Resort (Elysburg, Pennsylvania)

21. Hersheypark (Hershey, Pennsylvania)
22. Dutch Wonderland (Lancaster, Pennsylvania)
23. Kennywood (West Mifflin, Pennsylvania)
24. Six Flags Great America (Gurnee, Illinois)
25. Electric Park (Indianapolis, Indiana)
26. Adventureland (Des Moines, Iowa)
27. Boblo Island (Detroit, Michigan)
28. Michigan's Adventure (Muskegon, Michigan)
29. Knott's Camp Snoopy (Bloomington, Minnesota)
30. Valleyfair (Shakopee, Minnesota)
31. Silver Dollar City (Branson, Missouri)
32. Worlds of Fun (Kansas City, Missouri)
33. Six Flags Over Mid-America (St. Louis, Missouri)
34. Geauga Lake (Aurora, Ohio)
35. Paramount's Kings Island (Cincinnati, Ohio)
36. Cedar Point (Sandusky, Ohio)
37. Walt Disney World (Lake Buena Vista, Florida)
38. Busch Gardens, The Dark Continent (Tampa, Florida)
39. Six Flags Over Georgia (Atlanta, Georgia)
40. Paramount's Carowinds (Charlotte, North Carolina)
41. Ghost Town in the Sky (Maggie Valley, North Carolina)
42. Frontier City (Oklahoma City, Oklahoma)
43. Libertyland (Memphis, Tennessee)
44. Opryland USA (Nashville, Tennessee)
45. Dollywood (Pigeon Forge, Tennessee)
46. Wonderland Park (Amarillo, Texas)
47. Six Flags Over Texas (Arlington, Texas)
48. Astroworld (Houston, Texas)
49. Fiesta Texas (San Antonio, Texas)
50. Paramount's Kings Dominion (Doswell, Virginia)
51. Busch Gardens, The Old Country (Williamsburg, Virginia)
52. Disneyland (Anaheim, California)
53. Knott's Berry Farm (Buena Park, California)
54. Belmont Park (San Diego, California)
55. Paramount's Great America (Santa Clara, California)
56. Santa Cruz Beach Boardwalk (Santa Clara, California)
57. Six Flags Magic Mountain (Valencia, California)
58. West Edmonton Mall (Edmonton, Alberta, Canada)
59. Elitch Gardens (Denver, Colorado)
60. Lakeside (Denver, Colorado)
61. Silverwood Theme Park (Athol, Idaho)
62. Buffalo Bill's Wild West Resort (Las Vegas, Nevada)
63. Grand Slam Canyon (Las Vegas, Nevada)
64. Enchanted Forest (Turner, Oregon)
65. Lagoon (Farmington, Utah)
66. Puyallup Fair (Puyallup, Washington)

Location Guide to Amusement Parks and Roller Coasters

California

Disneyland
1313 Harbor Boulevard
Anaheim, California 92803

Opened in 1955, this was the first completely planned theme park. Today there are three themed roller coasters in the park.

Matterhorn (1959)
Designed by Arrow Dynamics, this was the first steel coaster using tubular tracks. The top of the Matterhorn is 146 feet high but the passenger cars only reach 80 feet before spiraling down, through and around the icy mountain, finishing with a splash as the cars hit the water at the base.

Space Mountain (1977)
Built after the success of Space Mountain in Walt Disney World, this Space Mountain is only slightly different. There is only one track and passengers sit side by side in these trains. The layout of the ride is similar to Disney World's but the ride is much smoother.

Big Thunder Mountain (1979)
This is the ultimate runaway mine train-type coaster. Much longer and more detailed than the others, it still uses tubular steel tracks.

Montezooma's Revenge
Opposite page, in less than 5 seconds, the coaster car on Montezooma's Revenge accelerates from 0–55 miles per hour, rides through a 76-foot-high loop, and zooms up a 140-foot-tall tower that ends in midair—then repeats the performance backward!

Roller Coasters Operating in North America

State/Province	Total	Wood	Steel
Alberta	3	0	3
Arizona	2	0	2
Arkansas	1	1	0
British Columbia	1	1	0
California	24	5	19
Colorado	4	3	1
Connecticut	1	1	0
Florida	6	1	5
Georgia	6	3	3
Idaho	1	0	1
Illinois	7	1	6
Indiana	2	1	1
Iowa	4	3	1
Kansas	1	1	0
Kentucky	3	1	2
Maryland	3	1	2
Massachusetts	4	3	1
Michigan	5	1	4
Minnesota	5	1	4
Missouri	7	2	5
Nevada	3	0	3
New Hampshire	3	1	2
New Jersey	10	2	8
New York	9	5	4
North Carolina	6	2	4
Nova Scotia	1	1	0
Ohio	20	8	12
Oklahoma	4	2	2
Ontario	7	2	5
Oregon	1	0	1
Pennsylvania	20	13	7
Quebec	3	1	2
Rhode Island	1	0	1
South Carolina	2	1	1
Tennessee	6	1	5
Texas	14	4	10
Utah	3	1	2
Virginia	8	3	5
Washington	1	1	0
West Virginia	2	1	1
Total	**214**	**79**	**135**

Knotts Berry Farm

8039 Beach Boulevard
Buena Park, California 90620

Knotts Berry Farm park opened in 1940 as Old West Ghost Town, near Walter Knott's Berry stand. Over the years more themed sections were added and the name was changed to Knotts Berry Farm.

Montezooma's Revenge (1978)

A shuttle loop-type coaster with a ride that takes a little over half a minute. It reaches 55 miles per hour before entering the 76-foot-high, 360-degree loop. It then runs to the top of the 148-foot high tower before stopping and returning backwards through the loop and to the station.

Boomerang
Below, the famous—or infamous—boomerang curve that gives the Knotts Berry Farm ride its name.

Boomerang (1990)

Designed by Vekoma International of The Netherlands, this coaster turns riders upside down six times in less than 1 minute. First pulled backwards up to the top of a nearly vertical eleven-story tower, the train is then released and attains 50 miles per hour, goes through a boomerang and a vertical loop, then heads up another nearly vertical eleven-story tower where the whole trip begins again—backwards.

The Steeplechase
Above, the Steeplechase at Coney Island was the inspiration for Arrow Dynamics' Wacky Soap Box Racers at Knotts Berry Farm.

Wacky Soap Box Racers (1980)

The only four-track (simultaneously running) coaster ride in the United States. You sit in individual cars like in that of a log flume, which ride along single tracks, banking into the turns as you race against the others at 30 miles per hour. This is a variation of the old Steeplechase roller coaster and quite a unique ride designed by Arrow Dynamics.

The original corkscrew designed by Arrow was located

at Knotts from 1975 to 1989. It was dismantled to make room for the new Boomerang and moved to Silverwood Theme Park in Coeur d'Alene, Idaho.

Belmont Park
3126 Mission Boulevard, Suite H
San Diego, California 92109

Located on Mission Beach, this was once the site of an amusement park that closed in 1976. Today there are shops, restaurants, and a completely restored roller coaster, which was also closed between 1976 and August 1990. There is also a small museum and gift shop devoted to roller coaster history and trivia, where tickets for the Giant Dipper are bought.

Giant Dipper (1925)
The revival of this classic wood-scaffold coaster was completed in August 1990. Originally designed by the renowned team of Frank Prior and Frederick Church, this is considered to be a sister of the Giant Dipper (1924) in Santa Cruz. Although that coaster was designed by Arthur Looff, Prior and Church patents were used on its planning. The Belmont Park coaster has tighter turns with steeper banks, however.

Paramounts Great America
PO Box 1776
Santa Clara, California 95052

Opened in 1976, this was originally one of the three Marriott theme parks.

The Grizzly (1986)
A 3200-foot-long wooden coaster based on the Wildcat, a coaster that ran from 1911 to 1964 at Coney Island in Cincinnati, Ohio. Its highest point is 90 feet and it has a top speed of 55 miles per hour during its 2-minute, 40-second run.

The Tidal Wave (1977)
A shuttle loop coaster that goes forward and then

Giant Dipper
Above, the Giant Dipper at Belmont Park is a classic woodie design with tightly banked turns.

The Tidal Wave
Above, built in 1977, The Tidal Wave continues to thrill riders today at Paramounts Great America.

backward along an 849-foot-long track. The train goes from 0–55 miles per hour in 4.2 seconds just before entering the 76-foot-high loop. The entire ride only takes 36 seconds.

The Tallest Roller Coasters in North America

There are a couple ways of determining the tallest roller coasters: 1. Sheer height of the lift or even the highest hill or loop; and 2. The longest drop, which can be even scarier than the height of the first lift. For instance, although Dorney Park's Hercules begins with a 95-foot lift, its first drop of 148 feet is spectacular, made possible due to the fact that the ride is built on the edge of a hill.

Height	Coaster	Material
209ft	The Desperado	steel
205ft	Magnum XL-200	steel
180ft	Rattler	wood
170ft	Shockwave	steel
160ft	The Mean Streak	wood
160ft	Steel Phantom	steel
148ft	Montezooma's Revenge	steel
143ft	Kumba	steel
143ft	Texas Giant	wood
141ft	The Beast	wood
140ft	Laser Loop	steel
132ft	Le Monstre	wood
130ft	Anaconda	steel
127ft	The American Eagle	wood

Drop	Coaster	Material
225ft	The Desperado	steel
225ft	Steel Phantom	steel
194ft	Magnum XL-200 (First hill)	steel
166ft	Rattler	wood
157ft	Magnum XL-200 (Second hill)	steel
155ft	Great American Scream Machine	steel
155ft	The Mean Streak	wood
148ft	Hercules	wood
145ft	Mindbender	steel
137ft	Texas Giant	wood
115ft	Orient Express	steel
114ft	The Loch Ness Monster	steel

The Demon (1980)

A steel coaster by Arrow Dynamics that has a lift height of 82 feet, two vertical loops of 70 and 55 feet, and a double corkscrew. The track is 1250 feet long with tunnels located along the way. Riding time is 1 minute, 45 seconds.

The Whizzer (1976)

A steel coaster by Anton Schwarzkopf that is 70 feet high and 3100 feet long with speeds of 42 miles per hour along 70-degree banked turns. This ride lasts for around 2 minutes.

Vortex (1991)

Designed by Bolliger & Mabillard of Switzerland, this is the only "stand-up" steel coaster west of the Mississippi. On this coaster, riders stand instead of sit as they follow a course at 45 miles per hour with the highlight being a 360-degree vertical loop.

The Demon
Above, the Demon was constructed in 1980 for Paramounts Great America.

Top Gun
Above, a suspended roller coaster, Top Gun opened at Paramounts Great America in 1993.

Top Gun (1993)

Bolliger & Mabillard designed this inverted coaster, which suspends the riders below the track. From a 100-foot lift the train takes off at 50 miles per hour along 2260

feet of track, going upside down on the outside of a vertical loop and corkscrew. The entire ride lasts 2 minutes, 26 seconds.

Top Gun
Above, the corkscrew on Top Gun spins riders upside down letting their feet dangle freely above their heads.

Santa Cruz Beach Boardwalk
400 Beach Street
Santa Cruz, California 95060

In bygone days, the Pacific Coast sported a string of boardwalks and amusement facilities. Then, one by one, the Pike in Long Beach, Playland in San Francisco, parks in Venice, Santa Monica, Portland, and San Diego, and the roller coasters these parks featured all disappeared. Santa

Cruz became a tourist attraction in 1865, when John Liebrandt built the first of many public bathhouses near the mouth of the San Lorenzo River, Bathhouse owners preached the health benefits of bathing in salt water to attract increasing numbers of tourists, who streamed into Santa Cruz using these facilities to change into swimsuits and enjoy the ocean's "natural medicine." Soon, concessions and a boardwalk patterned after the ones at Coney Island sprang up nearby.

Giant Dipper (1924)

Built in just 47 days at a cost of $50,000 this coaster is 1/2 mile long, a classic wooden twister, with graceful arches and sweeping fan curves that are surpassed only by the terror of its 70-foot drop and 55-miles-per-hour speeds. This structure was designed by Arthur Looff, who envisioned a giant wooden roller coaster that would be a "combination of earthquake, balloon ascension, and aeroplane drop." In 1987, the Giant Dipper was honored as a National Historic Landmark by the US National Park Service.

Hurricane (1992)

German designed and manufactured in Italy, this S. D. C. Windstorm steel coaster has a compact layout, which allows it to fit into the limited space of the boardwalk. It is described as unusually smooth for a coaster of its size, with 80-degree banked turns and twisting dives. The only other one like it in the United States is located in Long Island's Adventureland.

Viper
*Above, billed as "The Most
Frightening Ride on Earth,"
the Viper turns riders in the
28-passenger cars upside
down seven times along its
3830 feet of coiled steel
track. The $8 million coaster
features three vertical loops,
a corkscrew, and a head-over-
heels double loop called a
boomerang.*

Six Flags Magic Mountain
PO Box 5500
Valencia, California 91355

    The Six Flags Magic Mountain park opened in 1971.

Viper (1990)
    Designed by Arrow, this 3830-foot-long ride is the
world's largest looping steel roller coaster. It features three
360-degree loops, a double barrel boomerang, a classic
corkscrew, and an eighteen-story drop with speeds reaching 70 miles per hour, all during a 2 1/2 minute time span.

Ninja (1988)
    The first and only suspended coaster on the West Coast.
Arrow designed this 2700-foot-long, 2-minute ride with
angles up to 180 degrees and speeds of 55 miles per hour.

Revolution (1976)

The world's first giant looping roller coaster. Revolution is a smooth 3457-foot-long steel ride with one 360-degree vertical loop and a 144-foot-long tunnel, designed by Anton Schwarzkopf. The 2 1/2-minute ride has a top speed of 55 miles per hour and G-forces of 4.94 when entering the loop.

Colossus (1978)

At a top height of 115 feet, this is one of the tallest, longest, and fastest dual-track wooden roller coasters in the world. Designed by International Amusement Devices, Inc., the track is 4325 feet long and has 14 hills that are covered in 3 1/2 minutes at a top speed of 62 miles per hour.

Psyclone
Left, this classic woodie is a replica of New York's legendary Cyclone, built in 1927 at Coney Island and still regarded as the standard by which all other coasters are measured. Psyclone was constructed in 1991.

Gold Rusher (1971)

A runaway mine train-type roller coaster designed by Arrow Dynamics.

Psyclone (1991)

This is a classic wooden replica of the famous Coney Island Cyclone, designed by Curtis D. Summers. It begins with a 95-foot, 53-degree angled first drop and continues with five fan-banked turns, ten more drops and a 183-foot-long tunnel. The total ride takes 1 minute, 50 seconds and the fastest speed is 50 miles per hour.

Flashback
Right, originally opened in the early 1980s as Z-Force at Six Flags Over Georgia, the coaster was moved to Six Flags Magic Mountain and renamed Flashback.

Batman The Ride
Above, an inverted coaster, Batman The Ride opened in 1994 with movie props, sound effects, and more at Six Flags Magic Mountain's Gotham Backlot.

Flashback (1985)

This compact steel coaster designed by Intamin was originally built for Six Flags Great America, where it operated until 1988; then at Six Flags Over Georgia until 1991. It has a unique design that simulates flight by making six quick-turning vertical dives over a 1900-foot-long track. From a lift height of 86 feet, the train can reach speeds of 35 miles per hour during its 1 1/2-minute run.

Batman The Ride (1994)

Designed by Bolliger & Mabillard, this inverted coaster is 2700 feet long and includes two vertical outside loops and a twisting "Heartline Spin." From a 100-foot lift, the suspended train begins a 2-minute, 50-mile-per-hour ride through an area themed for *Batman: The Movie*.

Colorado

Elitch Gardens
4620 West 38th Avenue
Denver, Colorado 80212-2097

John and Mary Elitch opened their garden to the public in 1890, with P. T. Barnum and General and Mrs. Tom Thumb on hand for the festivities.

The Twister (1965)
Built by the Philadelphia Toboggan Company and supervised by John Allen, this coaster was re-engineered to increase speed in 1966. The classic wooden coaster is 3/4

The Twister
Above, building The Twister in 1965 required 362,505 board feet of wood—16 railroad box cars full!—11,262 pounds of nails, 16,649 bolts, and 3,648 gallons of paint in two coats.

The Wildcat
Left, this classic woodie was constructed in 1936 for Elitch Gardens.

The Wildcat
Above, a classic example of coaster architecture built by the Philadelphia Toboggan Company in 1927 for Lake Compounce Festival Park.

mile long with a height of 96 feet, 4 inches that gives riders a brief view of the Rocky Mountains just before plunging into a 63-mile-per-hour ride through a twisting course that includes a terrifying tunnel on a high-banked curve.

The Wildcat (1936)

A traditional camelback wooden coaster that interweaves with The Twister. It was also built by the Philadelphia Toboggan Company. 1993 is probably the last year of operation for this coaster as Elitch is moving to a new location in 1994.

Lakeside
4601 Sheridan Boulevard
Denver, Colorado 80212

Opened in 1908, Lakeside is a traditional amusement park with the roller coaster as the highlight.

The Cyclone (1940)

A traditional wooden coaster designed by Ed Vettel. From a 90-foot-tall lift, it takes just under 2 minutes to complete this 2800-foot-long twisting and turning track.

Connecticut

Lake Compounce Festival Park
822 Lake Avenue
Bristol, Connecticut 06010

Opened to the public in 1846 with walking paths, a bandstand, picnic tables, and rowboats. A trolley line was brought to the park in 1896. The first coaster was built in 1914 (Green Dragon) but was replaced in 1927.

The Wildcat (1927)

Built by the Philadelphia Toboggan Company, this coaster is a classic example of the Golden Age of coaster architecture. It was completely refurbished in 1985 by Charles Dinn. The deteriorated wood was replaced, board for board, with pressure treated, long leaf yellow pine, and 3000 feet of steel-banded track. Though a small coaster by today's standards, the combination of wood and two high-bank fan curves makes for a fast-paced, intense ride. The first drop is 78–80 feet high and the riding time is only 52 seconds.

Florida

Walt Disney World
PO Box 10100
Lake Buena Vista, Florida 32830-0100

Opened in 1971, this complete resort includes the Magic Kingdom, a park modeled after Disneyland. Currently there are only two themed tubular steel track coasters in the park, but rumors are that there is a "classic" wooden roller coaster being designed for a new Boardwalk attraction that is under development. Also, EPCOT Center will soon have a Switzerland pavilion complete with a Matterhorn bobsled coaster similar to the one at Disneyland.

Space Mountain (1975)
Located in the Tomorrowland section, this cone-shaped structure rises to a height of 183 feet and encompasses 4,508,500 cubic feet of dark, mysterious space. Passengers board rocket shuttles that climb high into space before beginning the descent along an intricate twisting complex of guideways.

Big Thunder Mountain Railroad (1980)
This is the ultimate runaway mine train-type of roller coaster. Each train carries up to thirty adult passengers along 2780 feet of track, past sandstone buttes and windswept canyons, through a booming Gold Rush town, and into the Big Thunder Mine.

Busch Gardens, The Dark Continent
PO Box 9158
Tampa, Florida 33674

One of the Anheuser-Busch Companies, this park is themed and dedicated to animal wildlife. Among the many attractions are three exciting steel coasters.

Python
*Right, built in 1976, Python is
still thrilling riders today at
Busch Gardens, The Dark
Continent.*

Python (1976)

This is a 1250-feet-long classic tubular steel corkscrew designed by Arrow Dynamics. The train can reach
a top speed of 50 miles per hour at the bottom of a 70-
foot drop before entering the double corkscrew at 27
miles per hour. The complete ride takes 1 minute, 10
seconds.

Scorpion (1981)

This is an Anton Schwarzkopf coaster that rides for 2
minutes, 15 seconds. The 1805-foot-long steel track has a
first lift of 65 feet and a drop of 62 feet giving it a speed
of 50 miles per hour before entering the one vertical loop.
In this loop a person feels the pull of 3.5 G's.

Scorpion
Left, the 360-degree loop at Busch Gardens cuts through the trees, accentuating the feeling of careening upside down.

Kumba
Left, four riders set abreast in each car of the Kumba coaster. Kumba was constructed in 1993 for Busch Gardens, The Dark Continent.

Kumba
Above, Kumba features four inversions during its hair-raising 2-minute, 38-second ride over 3900 feet of track.

Kumba (1993)

Sitting four across, passengers plunge into the world's largest vertical loop—108 feet high!—from a 143-foot-high lift. Bolliger & Mabillard designed this 2-minute, 54-second ride, which covers 3978 feet of track at speeds of 60 miles per hour. The name "Kumba" means "roar" in the African Congo language, which is appropriate for this looping, spiraling coaster that at times pulls 3.75 G's.

Georgia

Six Flags Over Georgia
PO Box 43187
Atlanta, Georgia 30378

This park opened around 1967 just to the west of Atlanta as the second of several parks that the company now operates.

Georgia Cyclone (1990)
Designed by Curtis D. Summers, this is the South's only twister-type coaster. It was patterned after the legendary Coney Island Cyclone. With a 95-foot lift and a 78 1/2-foot drop at a 53-degree angle, this coaster twists inside and out, while racing around high-banked turns along the 2970-feet-long course. It has been described as a 10-acre ride on a 3-acre site, all packed into 1 minute, 48 seconds.

The Great American Scream Machine
Left, lit up by lights and fireworks, a nighttime ride on a coaster is a completely different experience from a daytime ride. The Great American Scream Machine was constructed in 1973 for Six Flags Over Georgia.

The Great American Scream Machine (1973)

This is a 3800-foot-long wooden out-and-back designed by John Allen of the Philadelphia Toboggan Company. The first drop is 87 feet from a 105-foot-high lift. The ride takes 2 minutes.

Mind Bender (1978)

The first triple-looping steel coaster in North America. Designed by Anton Schwarzkopf, this ride takes 2 minutes, 33 seconds and has a lift hill of 80 feet followed by vertical loops that are 56 feet tall.

Ninja (1992)

This 2900-foot-long, 110-foot-high steel coaster was formerly the Kamikaze (1989) at Hunts Pier, which is now called Conko's Party Pier, located in New Jersey. It has five inversions: corkscrew, sidewinder, and butterfly loop in a compact layout designed by Vekoma.

Dahlonega Mine Train (1967)

Developed by Arrow, this 2323-foot-long runaway mine train is themed for the early Gold Rush days in the northern Georgia town of Dahlonega. As a sidenote, it was in reference to this location that the statement, "There's gold in them thar hills," was made.

Idaho

Silverwood Theme Park

N26225 Highway 95
Athol, Idaho 83801

This park is the home of the first coaster to successfully take riders upside down in the modern era.

Gravity Defying Corkscrew (1975)

Moved here in 1990 from Knott's Berry Farm, this is Arrow Dynamics' original corkscrew coaster. The 1-minute, 10-second ride begins with a 70-foot-high lift and covers 1250 feet of track while at times reaching speeds of 45 miles per hour.

Gravity Defying Corkscrew
Opposite page, this Idaho ride lives up to its name. Constructed in 1975 for Knotts Berry Farm, this was Arrow Dynamics' first upside-down roller coaster, featuring two 360 degree loops through which passengers are carried at speeds of up to 45 miles per hour. The coaster was moved to Silverwood Theme Park in Coeur D'Alene, Idaho.

Shockwave

Right, Shockwave was constructed in 1988 for Six Flags Great America. From the start, the cars climb a 170-foot lift hill, soar down a 155-foot banking drop, and race through seven loops.

The Whizzer

Above, the Whizzer at Six Flags Great America is built around fast spiral-shaped, high-banked turns.

The American Eagle

Above, the Eagle is a twin-track woodie racer constructed in 1981 and located at Six Flags Great America.

Illinois

Six Flags Great America
PO Box 1776
Gurnee, Illinois 60031

Great America opened in 1976 and was one of three amusement parks owned by the Marriott Corporation. The park is now part of the Six Flags family.

Shockwave (1988)
Designed by Arrow Dyamics, this steel coaster starts at a height of 170 feet and moves down a 155-foot, 55-degree angle—that banks as well—into a total of seven loops. It contains two 116-foot and one 130-foot vertical high loops, a double corkscrew, and a boomerang. It takes about 2 minutes, 20 seconds to cover the 3900-foot-long track with a top speed of 65 miles per hour.

The American Eagle (1981)
Twin wooden racing coaster designed by Intamin, Inc. It is 4650 feet long and has a lift of 127 feet. The first drop is at a 55-degree angle and the top recorded speed is 66.32 miles per hour.

The Demon (1976)

A steel coaster by Arrow Dyamics, it has a height of 82 feet, two vertical loops of 70 and 55 feet in height, and a double corkscrew. The track is 1250 feet long with three mysterious tunnels. Riding time is 1 minute, 45 seconds.

Tidal Wave (1978)

This is a shuttle loop coaster by Anton Schwarzkopf with a 76-foot-high vertical loop and a total track length of 849 feet. The train goes from 0–55 miles per hour within 5 seconds. This causes the first car into the loop to reach 6.0 G's with the average car feeling 2.0 G's. The train moves through the loop and up a hill, stops for an instant, then returns to the station backwards.

The Whizzer (1976)

A steel coaster by Anton Schwarzkopf, The Whizzer is 70 feet high, 3100 feet long with speeds of 42 miles per hour along the 70-degree banked turns. This ride lasts for 2 minutes.

Iron Wolf (1990)

By Bolliger & Mabillard, this is the United States' largest and fastest "stand-up" looping coaster. Riders stand instead of sitting as they are propelled through more than a half mile of track packed with steep drops, two tight curves, and two 360-degree loops. It is 100 feet high, 2900 feet long with a 90-foot-high first drop. It has a top speed of 55 miles per hour and a ride time of 2 minutes.

Batman The Ride (1992)

Designed by Bolliger & Mabillard, this 2700-foot-long prototype is the world's first inverted outside looping roller coaster. Because the cars are not allowed to swing like that of a traditional suspended coaster, it was possible to take vertical loops on the "outside" of the loop. In fact, there are a total of five inversions: two vertical loops, two flatspins (corkscrews), and a unique heartline spin that is a roll designed to give the sensation of 0 G's for about 4 seconds. Statistically, the coaster has a high point of 100 feet, a vertical loop of 77 feet, and speeds up to 50 miles per hour during the 2-minute ride. Another unique characteristic is the chair-lift-type seat where your feet dangle below, as if you are on a swing. To market this new coaster concept, the

Tidal Wave
Above, the Tidal Wave at Six Flags Great America features a 55-mile-per-hour trip through a 76-foot-high vertical loop—and then repeats the trip backward.

Batman The Ride
Above, six flags Great America's Batman The Ride was the first suspended, outside-looping coaster.

name was chosen by Six Flags (Time-Warner) to coincide with the Warner Bros. movie release of *Batman Returns*.

Indiana

Electric Park
(Proposed)

The park is to be located on a 50-acre site 28 miles south of Indianapolis, Indiana. The idea of the park is to preserve the amusement park era of 1890–1960, including the rides, games, and architecture of that time. One area would have the Coney Island flavor of 1900–1930; another, the Art Deco style of the 1940s and 1950s. Among the twenty major rides the park will open with is a priceless gondola carousel (circa 1890) made in Germany's Black Forest and donated by Opryland. This is the only one of its kind in the country.

Wild Cat (1929)
Designed by the Philadelphia Toboggan Company, this coaster was donated by Idora Park, where it ran until 1983.

Flying Turns
This is a cousin of the coaster in which three-wheeled cars are pulled to the top of a hill and then released bobsled style down a cypress-wood track.

Iowa

Adventureland
PO Box 3355
Des Moines, Iowa 50316

The park is themed on the history of Iowa, including a turn-of-the-century main street full of architectural replicas.

Tornado (1979)
From a 93-foot-high lift, this 2840-foot-long coaster can reach 58 miles per hour during its 2-minute out-and-back run. This wooden coaster was designed by William Cobb.

Iron Wolf
Opposite page, this stand-up coaster at Six Flags Great America travels through a 360-degree loop, hairpin turns, a corkscrew loop, and drops down cliff-like slopes at speeds up to 55 miles per hour.

Wild One
Right, the Wild One at Wild World is a classic woodie, built in 1917.

Dragon (1990)

O. D. Hopkins Associates, Inc., built this 2250-foot-long double-looping coaster. It has a 90-foot-high lift with an 85-foot drop and runs for 1 minute, 30 seconds.

The Outlaw (1993)

The 2800-foot-long wooden twister designed by Custom Coaster, Inc., incorporates nine drops and twelve turns in its course. The highest point is the 67-foot-high lift.

Maryland

Wild World

13710 Central Avenue
PO Box 1610
Mitchellville, Maryland 20716

The Wild World amusement park opened in 1982.

Wild One (1917)

Formerly the Giant at Paragon Park, this coaster was moved to Wild World and made its debut in 1986. This 4000-foot-long woodie was originally designed and built by John Miller and the Philadelphia Toboggan Company. The lift hill is 98 feet high and the track drops at a 52-degree angle to begin the 2-minute ride at 55 miles per hour. This coaster was once the longest and highest in New England and was well known in the Boston area for its history since it was a favorite of local and national celebrities. The Kennedys, Judy Garland, and Ted Williams all rode the coaster numerous times and Boston's Cardinal Cushing celebrated his birthday on the Giant coaster each year.

Massachusetts

Riverside Amusement Park

Box 307
Agawam, Massachusetts 01001

This is a traditional amusement park that got its start in 1840 as a picnic grove called "Gallups Grove." In the late 1880s, the name was changed to "Riverside Grove" before being shortened to just "Riverside" in 1912. It was at this time that Riverside Amusement Park began to evolve into New England's largest.

Riverside Cyclone (1983)

Designed by William Cobb, this coaster has been called the most bone-jarring, harrowing ride in America. Although it does not set any records, the 3600 feet of track represents sheer terror. It is built in a small area, requiring steeper drops and quicker turns. The lift hill has a 28-degree slope and the first drop takes the train from 0–60

miles per hour in just 3 seconds down a 54-degree banked twisting fall into a 60-degree high-speed bank turn.

Black Widow (1977)

On this Arrow Dynamics-designed steel shuttle loop, the train is launched forward down a 50-foot drop at 45 miles per hour into a 360-degree loop before stopping at a second "launchpad." The trip is then repeated—backwards!

Thunderbolt (1941)

Originally named the Cyclone, the coaster was designed from original blueprints used to build the coaster for the 1939 New York World's Fair. This wooden classic is 70 feet high, 2865 feet long, and runs for 60 seconds.

The Longest Roller Coasters in North America

There are three ways to measure the longest roller coasters: 1. Sheer length of ride in terms of the track; 2. The time the ride takes from start to finish; and 3. The imagined length of the ride due to the sheer terror it induces. Here's a look at the first two; the third only you can determine for yourself.

Length	Coaster	Material
7400ft	The Beast	wood
5900ft	The Desperado	steel
5427ft	The Mean Streak	wood
5106ft	Magnum XL-200	steel
5080ft	Rattler	wood
4920ft	Texas Giant	wood
4650ft	The American Eagle	wood
4601ft	Colossus	wood
4230ft	Timber Wolf	wood
4198ft	Mindbender	steel
4000ft	Wild One	wood
3990ft	Le Monstre	wood

Time	Coaster	Material
4 min, 30 sec	The Beast	wood
3 min, 30 sec	Colossus	wood
3 min, 30 sec	Ripsaw	steel
3 min	The Desperado	steel
3 min	Dragon Mountain	steel
3 min	XLR-8	steel
3 min	The Big Bad Wolf	steel
2 min, 54 sec	Kumba	steel
2 min, 50 sec	Batman The Ride	steel
2 min, 42 sec	Cedar Creek Mine Ride	steel
2 min, 40 sec	Grizzly	wood

Whalom Park

Route 13
Fitchburg, Massachusetts 01420

Whalom Park is a traditional amusement park, located about 45 miles west of Boston. Since 1893, the people of New England have attended this park for the beaches, boating, and picnic facilities. It is also home to a classic Philadelphia Toboggan Company coaster.

Flyer Comet (1940)
This is a classic wooden figure-eight, designed by the Philadelphia Toboggan Company. With a 70-foot-tall lift hill, the train can achieve a maximum speed of 35 miles per hour. Although the ride is not of great length, it represents a link to the past.

Michigan

Michigan's Adventure
4850 Whitehall Road
Muskegon, MI 49445

The Screamer
Below, built in 1985, The Screamer is located at Boblo Island.

A traditional amusement park that is the home of Michigan's only wooden coaster.

Corkscrew (1979)

This is one of Arrow Dynamics' basic corkscrew designs: 70 feet high, 1250 feet long, and a top speed of 45 miles per hour.

Wolverine Wildcat (1988)

A 3000-foot-long natural-colored wooden double-out-and-back designed and built by Curtis D. Summers and Charles Dinn. This 2-minute ride begins from an 85-foot-high lift and reaches a top speed of 55 miles per hour.

Flyer Comet
Above, the Flyer Comet was built in 1940 at Whalom Park.

Boblo Island

4401 W. Jefferson
Detroit, Michigan 48209

Boblo's original name was Etiowiteedannenti, a name coined by the Huron Indians who once lived there. Due to its strategic location, several different people have occupied the island. It was the French who renamed the island "Bois Blanc," meaning white wood, for the trees that stood there. Boblo first opened as a recreational destination in 1898 as a picnic and park area. Unable to pronounce Bois Blanc, visitors began calling the island Boblo. The name was officially adopted in 1929.

The Screamer (1985)

A classic tubular steel double corkscrew designed by Vekoma.

The Nightmare (1988)

An enclosed roller coaster by Vekoma that provides visitors with a thrilling 90-second ride through darkness on an 1150-foot-long track.

Sky Streak (1973)

A 2500-foot-long steel out-and-back by the Sansi Corporation of Japan.

Minnesota

Knott's Camp Snoopy

Mall of America
Bloomington, Minnesota 55425

Operation of this indoor amusement park began in 1992 as part of the nation's largest shopping center, Mall of America. The park was created by Knott's Berry Farm as the centerpiece to Bloomington's mega-mall, which was developed by the builders of the West Edmonton Mall in Canada.

Ripsaw (1992)

This coaster was designed by Zierer to be a milder family type of ride, electrically driven through 2500 feet of

High Roller
Below, a classic woodie, High Roller was constructed in 1976 for Valleyfair in Shakopee, Minnesota.

track. The entire ride lasts for 3 1/2 minutes and reaches a top speed of 30 miles per hour at a maximum height of 60 feet above the ground—all within the Mall of America's center courtyard.

Valleyfair
One Valleyfair Drive
Shakopee, Minnesota 55379

The Valleyfair park opened in 1976.

High Roller (1976)
Designed by International Amusement Service, Inc. of Dayton, Ohio, this is a 2982-foot-long wooden out-and-back L-shaped course. It has a 70-foot-high lift and a ride time of 1 minute, 45 seconds with a top speed of 50 miles per hour.

Wildrails (1979)
Created by Anton Schwarzkopf of Germany, Wildrails features a 50-foot-high steel figure-eight with spirals. Individual cars, which seat four, reach speeds of 40–50 miles per hour along a 1054-foot-long track. The entire ride lasts 1 minute, 34 seconds.

Corkscrew (1980)
Created by Arrow Dynamics, Corkscrew is a steel double corkscrew coaster that is 85 feet high and 1950 feet long.

Excalibur (1989)
A wooden structure with tubular steel track designed by Arrow Dynamics, Excalibur is 105 feet high with a 60-degree first drop and has eight track crisscrosses along the 2415-foot-long course. The ride lasts 2 minutes, 17 seconds and reaches a top speed of 55 miles per hour.

Excalibur
Above, a thoroughly modern steel-track coaster, Excalibur was built in 1989 for Valleyfair.

Missouri

Silver Dollar City
Branson, Missouri 65616

Themed as an 1890s mountain mining community, this park opened in 1960 and is primarily a crafts showplace.

Thunderation
Above, the ultimate in runaway trains, Thunderation at Silver Dollar City is a runaway steam train headed by this locomotive.

Thunderation (1993)

Designed by Arrow Dynamics, this 3022-foot-long coaster is a runaway mine train type that begins with an 81-foot-high lift and runs for 2 minutes, 10 seconds at 48 miles per hour. It includes 60-degree banked turns and a 79-degree double helix.

Worlds of Fun

4545 Worlds of Fun Avenue
Kansas City, Missouri 64161

The Worlds of Fun park opened in 1973.

Orient Express (1980)

A steel coaster that features interlocking loops and a Kamikaze Kurve (the world's first boomerang), a ride innovation that turns passengers upside down in each of two barrel rolls within 13 seconds. The ride is 3470 feet long with a first drop of 115 feet at a 55-degree angle. It has five drops in all, and a top speed of 65 miles per hour. In addition, this Arrow Dynamics design, which lasts 2 minutes, 30 seconds, has a 100-foot-long tunnel. The ride reaches a reported G-force of 3.5.

Timber Wolf (1989)

Designed by Curtis D. Summers, this wooden coaster is ten stories tall with a 95 foot drop. It speeds along the 4230-foot-long track with hairpin turns and an unusual 560-degree helix at 53 miles per hour. The ride lasts for about 2 1/2 minutes.

Zambezi Zinger (1973)

Created by Anton Schwarzkopf, this is a 2100-foot-long

Orient Express
Above, over 11.3 million riders rode the Orient Express at Worlds of Fun in the first ten years of its operation. The ride features a 115-foot drop.

Timber Wolf
Above, this Worlds of Fun woodie was built in 1989.

steel coaster with an electrically powered spiral ascent to a drop, which achieves a top speed of 40 miles per hour. The ride entails a series of hills and banks—up to 55 degrees—fitting into the natural terrain, along with a tunnel. It is a smooth, swift ride with sharp tree-top turns that is intensified at night.

Six Flags Over Mid-America
Box 666
Eureka, Missouri 63025

This Six Flags park opened in 1971.

The Screamin' Eagle (1976)
It was built as the world's longest, tallest, and fastest. It is 110 feet high, 3872 feet long, and originally had a top speed of 62 miles per hour. Designed by John Allen and engineered by Bill Cobb, the ride features a unique "swoop curve" that slows the cars momentarily before plunging them down the track's first 87 foot precipice and into their 62 miles per hour ride only to climb to the ride's highest point for a second dive 92 feet straight down.

In 1990, new, faster cars replaced the older ones and increased the speeds from 62 miles per hour to 70 miles per hour. The major contribution to the increased speed comes from the fact that each car, with the exception of the lead car, only has two sets of wheels versus four, thereby creating less friction and less resistance on the track. Quick acceleration and a sense of weightlessness is caused by the space tolerance allowed between the top and bottom wheels. With the absence of the second set of wheels, the floating sensation that riders experience when careening down the Screamin' Eagle's steep hills is now intensified.

Ninja (1989)
A steel coaster designed by Vekoma Ride Manufacturing that takes riders upside down four times. At 2430 feet long and 110 feet high, the ride has a top speed of 65 miles per hour. This coaster was originally located in Vancouver, Canada, as part of the World's Fair in 1986 before being dismantled and moved to Six Flags.

The Screamin' Eagle
Left, a classic-style woodie, The Screamin' Eagle was built in 1976 and is located at Six Flags Over Mid-America.

Ninja
Below, billed as "The Black Belt of Roller Coasters," Ninja at Six Flags Over Mid-America features 2430 feet of track running at speeds up to 65 miles per hour with high-speed spirals, a double corkscrew, a 360-degree clothoid loop, and a sidewinder.

River King Mine Train (1971)

Another mine train type of coaster installed during the early seventies and designed by Arrow Dynamics. This was the original coaster of Six Flags (actually there were two, but one was sold to Dollywood).

Nevada

Buffalo Bill's Wild West Resort
I-15 South Stateline
PO Box 95997
Las Vegas, Nevada 89193-5997

Located at the California-Nevada border on I-15, this western-themed Hotel-Casino includes the world's tallest roller coaster among other attractions.

The Desperado (1994)

At a lift height of 209 feet, this Arrow Dyamics-designed steel coaster beats out Magnum XL-200 by 4 feet for the honor of the worlds tallest. The 5900-foot-long, 3-minute experience also ties Steel Phantom for the longest drop at 225 feet and top speed of 80 miles per hour.

Circus Circus
2880 Las Vegas Boulevard South
Las Vegas, Nevada 89109-1120

Opening in 1993, this 5-acre amusement park all contained within a gigantic pink glass dome initiated the new Vegas image of a "family" destination.

Canyon Blaster (1993)

This 2423-foot-long double-looping corkscrew layout was designed by Arrow Dynamics. It has a first drop of 66 feet from a lift of 94 feet and a top speed of 41 miles per hour during the 1-minute ride.

Canyon Blaster
Above, built in 1993, Canyon Blaster is one of just a few American coasters constructed within an enclosed building—in this case, Grand Slam Canyon, located directly behind Circus Circus on the Las Vegas strip.

New Hampshire

Canobie Lake Park
PO Box 190
Salem, New Hampshire 03079

This park opened in 1902 as a street car (railway) amusement facility.

The Yankee Cannonball (1930)
This coaster was originally built by the Philadelphia Toboggan Company for Lakewood Park in Waterbury, Connecticut. In 1936, it was purchased by Canobie Lake Park and moved. It is a wooden out-and-back. It is about 2000 feet long and has a first drop of 63 1/2 feet. With a top speed of 35 miles per hour, the ride lasts a little less than 2 minutes. In 1954, Hurricane Carol demolished the first hill, but it was repaired. In 1976, a fire destroyed the station, yet this classic coaster, which the late John Allen proclaimed as the smoothest riding of his day, continues to roll on.

Canobie Corkscrew (1975)
Originally operated in Old Chicago and the Alabama State Fair before being moved here in 1990. Designed by Arrow Dyamics.

New Jersey

Clementon Amusement Park
Box 125
Clementon, New Jersey 08021

Clementon remains as the last of the great turn-of-the-century amusement parks in the Philadelphia area. It has been owned and operated by the same family since its beginning.

Jack Rabbit (1919)
Designed by John Miller, this is the second oldest Philadelphia Toboggan coaster still operating. The wooden figure-eight is 1380 feet in length with a lift of 50 feet. It is basically a side-friction coaster with no under-wheels.

Six Flags Great Adventure
PO Box 120
Jackson, New Jersey 08527

Called America's largest seasonal theme park, this area also includes a drive-through safari full of wild animals. One of Marriott's three parks at one time, it is now a part of the Six Flags family.

Runaway Train (1973)
One of Arrow Dynamics' mine train coasters, the tubular steel track provides for a smooth family-type ride.

The Great American Scream Machine
Below, located at Six Flags Great Adventure, The Great American Scream Machine was constructed in 1989.

Rolling Thunder (1979)
Designed by Don Rosser and engineered by William Cobb, this wooden twin-track out-and-back is 3200 feet long and has a lift hill of 96 feet. Its top speed of 56 miles per hour occurs as the train reaches the bottom of the first drop.

Rolling Thunder
Left, Rolling Thunder is a classic-style twin-track racer woodie, built in 1979 and located at Six Flags Great Adventure.

Lightnin' Loops (1978)

Twin shuttle loop coasters designed by Arrow Dynamics. The steel track vertical loop is the highlight of the ride as a train that is propelled from the station enters it twice—once forward and once backward on its return.

Great American Scream Machine (1989)

Arrow Dynamics designed this steel coaster with seven inversions: three vertical loops, a double corkscrew, and a boomerang. The track is 3800 feet long and has a lift height of 173 feet. The train can reach 68 miles per hour during its 155 foot first drop on a ride lasting 2 minutes, 20 seconds.

Runaway Train
Above, constructed in 1973, Runaway Train is one of Arrow Dynamics classic runaway mine train coasters, located at Six Flags Great Adventure.

Batman The Ride (1993)

A Bolliger & Mabillard inverted coaster 2693 feet in length with five inversions including two vertical outside loops, two outside helices, and a zero-gravity roll. The 2-minute, 50-miles-per-hour ride starts from a 105-foot-high lift.

New York

Astroland

1000 Surf Avenue
Coney Island, New York 11224

The world-famous Cyclone has been a part of this park since 1975. In July 1977, *Town and Country* magazine called this classic the perfect roller coaster: "It never stops or slows for a second after it leaves the lift. Its drops, turns, and twists are unsurpassed in the coaster world and it is as smooth and graceful as a seagull. New Yorkers should consider the Cyclone as valuable as the Statue of Liberty or the Empire State Building."

Cyclone (1927)

Designed by Vernan Keenan and built by Harry C. Baker, this coaster required an initial investment of $175,000. The lift hill is 85 feet high and drops at a 60-degree angle, which pushes the train to 60 miles per hour. The 3000-foot-long track also includes six fan turns and nine drops. The entire ride lasts for 1 minute, 50 seconds. Charles Lindbergh once said that the thrill of the Cyclone even beat the thrill of flying.

Darien Lake

Theme Park and Camping Resort
Darien Center, New York 14040

This park opened in 1980 and is owned by Funtime, Inc., which also operates Geauga Lake Park in Aurora, Ohio, and Wyandot Lake Park in Columbus, Ohio.

Predator (1990)

Designed by Curtis D. Summers, this is New York's largest wooden roller coaster. The 2-minute ride is laid out

Cyclone
Above, the legendary Cyclone at Astroland in New York's Coney Island is the roller coaster that all others are judged against. Cyclone opened in 1927 and has thrilled millions of riders through the years. Brooklyn Public Library

Cyclone
Opposite page, the Cyclone continues to scare riders today. The classic 1927 woodie is still running strong at Astroland in Coney Island.

Predator
Above, constructed in 1990, Predator is located at Darien Lake.

in an L-shape that crosses through itself, with a lot of action on the curves. This ride has very few straight sections and a total of twelve drops. It is 3400 feet long and 99 feet high.

The Viper (1982)

This is a steel coaster by Arrow Dynamics that has a series of five upside-down turns. Down a 75 foot drop within 4 seconds, the train reaches 50 miles per hour and enters the vertical loop followed by a double corkscrew and a boomerang curve.

The Great Escape

PO Box 511
Lake George, New York 12845

A traditional amusement park that opened in 1955.

The Viper
Above, Darien Lake's Viper runs over a half mile of steel and five upside-down turns.

Steamin' Demon (1978)

This is a classic steel track corkscrew designed by Arrow Dynamics, which was moved here in 1984 from Pontchartrain Beach in New Orleans.

Comet (1947)

The Comet one consistently ranks among the top ten roller coasters by enthusiasts. Located in Crystal Beach park until 1989, this famous wooden coaster was designed by the Philadelphia Toboggan Company.

Seabreeze

4600 Culver Road
Rochester, New York 14622

Over the long history of this park, which opened in 1879, there have been six coasters located here. The Figure-Eight (1903), the Greyhound (1918), the Jack Rabbit (1920), the Virginia Reel (1921), the Wildcat (1922), and the Bobsleds (1968). Two of these remain today. The park also has a historical museum on the grounds that contains information on these coasters as well as a special exhibit called "Coast to Coast Coasters."

Jack Rabbit (1920)

This is a wooden modified figure-eight designed by the Philadelphia Toboggan Company. The first lift is 75 feet high and the track is 2130 feet long with a 265-foot-long tunnel along the way.

Bobsleds (1968)

Designed by George W. Long, this 1240-foot-long coaster is constructed of wood with tubular steel track.

Playland Park

Playland Parkway
Rye, New York 10580

Opening in 1928, Playland was America's first totally planned amusement park and the prototype for today's theme parks. It was completely and carefully planned as a family park by the Westchester County Park Commission. Today, it has its place on the National Register of Historic Places and is managed by the Department of Parks, Recreation and Conservation.

From 1928 to 1957, this was the home of the famous Aeroplane Coaster designed by Fred Church. This 3600-

Thunder Road
Right, Thunder Road is themed after the Robert Mitchum moonshine-running movie Thunder Road. Construction of the roller coaster in 1976 at Paramount's Carowinds required 539,000 board feet of lumber, 30,000 bolts, 3,500 pounds of nails, and 5,500 gallons of paint.

foot-long coaster was named in honor of Lindbergh's flight in 1927 and was similar to the Bobs-style coaster at Chicago's Riverview Park. It has been called the "greatest body wringer and most violent ride ever built."

Dragon Coaster (1929)

Another wooden thriller designed by Fred Church, it is 80 feet high and 3400 feet long. This 2-minute ride gives the impression of being hurled into the mouth of a dragon.

North Carolina

Paramount's Carowinds
PO Box 410289
Charlotte, North Carolina 28241

Located on the border between North and South Carolina, Carowinds first opened in 1973. This park offers a unique atmosphere that is rich in Carolina heritage and full of Southern hospitality.

Thunder Road (1976)

This is a wooden twin-racing coaster that is 3819 feet long and has a lift hill of 93 feet. Designed by John Allen, the ride takes 2 minutes, 10 seconds to complete, reaching a top speed of 58 miles per hour while averaging 42 miles per hour.

Carolina Cyclone (1980)

This is an Arrow Dynamics-designed steel quadruple-looping roller coaster. There are two consecutive 360-degree vertical loops followed by two consecutive 360-degree barrel rolls (corkscrew), and a 450-degree uphill helix.

Carolina Cyclone
Above, built in 1980, the Carolina Cyclone is located at Paramount's Carowinds.

Vortex
Above, Carowinds' stand-up coaster runs over 2040 feet of steel track.

Vortex
Right, the Vortex is Carowinds' stand-up coaster. It cost $5.5 million to construct.

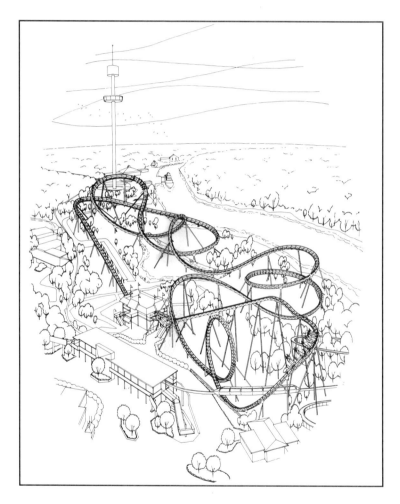

Goldrusher (1972)

The original coaster of the park designed by Arrow as a runaway mine train type.

Vortex (1992)

Designed by Bolliger & Mabillard of Switzerland, this coaster is a one-of-a-kind found only at Carowinds. Although there are other "stand-up" steel coasters, this is the first to provide an oblique loop as well as a vertical loop and a "flat-spin." Statistically, the track is 2040 feet long with a 90-foot-tall lift that pushes the train to a top speed of 50 miles per hour. Each train holds 24 passengers, with every coach holding four people standing side by side. This shorter train (three cars) reduces the different experiences of riding in the front and the back. All of these elements make the Vortex a unique ride for which designer Claude Mabillard declared "the best coaster Bolliger & Mabillard has built up to now."

Red Devil
Above, Ghost Town in the Sky's Red Devil was built in 1988.

The Hurler (1994)

Designed by International Coaster, Inc., this 3157-foot-long woodie is themed for the "Wayne's World" section. From an 83 foot lift the train can reach a top speed of 50 miles per hour during its 2-minute run.

Ghost Town in the Sky

PO Box 369
US 19
Maggie Valley, NC 28751

Located on 275 acres in the Smokey Mountains, this park has several carnival rides and one coaster.

Red Devil (1988)

One of the first coasters designed by O. D. Hopkins Association, Inc. A single-looping 2037-foot-long ride with a top speed of 50 miles per hour. The unusual part of this coaster is that the 90-foot-high lift is not reached until the end of the 2-minute run.

Ohio

Geauga Lake

1060 Aurora Road
Aurora, Ohio 44202

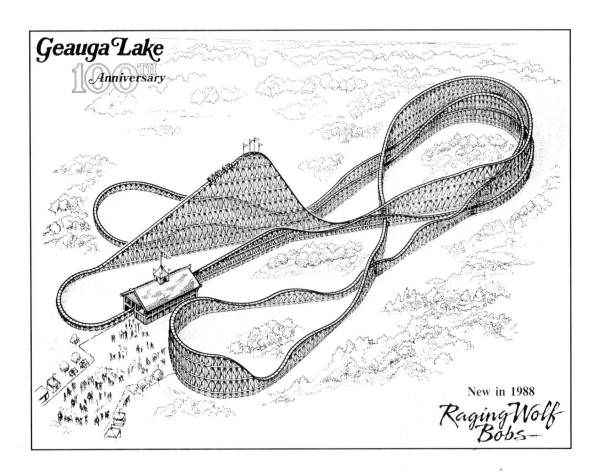

Geauga Lake
100TH Anniversary

New in 1988
Raging Wolf Bobs

The Geauga Lake park has operated since 1888.

The Raging Wolf Bobs (1988)

A wooden coaster inspired by the infamous wooden Riverview Bobs at Riverview Park in Chicago, IL (1924–1967). This coaster is 80 feet high and over a half a mile long. Speeds reach 50 miles per hour and some curves are banked up to 55 degrees. Riding time is approximately 2 minutes.

The Big Dipper (1926)

This old wooden coaster, designed by John Miller, was completely overhauled in 1980. It is 65 feet high, 2680 feet long, and has a top speed of only 32 miles per hour. The total ride time is 1 minute, 45 seconds.

Double Loop (1977)

Designed by Arrow Dynamics, this was America's first

double-looping coaster. This steel coaster is 95 feet high, 1800 feet long, and has a top speed of 36 miles per hour.

Corkscrew (1978)

This is a classic Arrow Dynamics design of tubular steel track, 75 feet high and 1250 feet long.

Paramount's Kings Island

Kings Island, Ohio 45034

This park opened in 1972 after the century-old Coney Island amusement park, which was located on the banks of the Ohio River in Cincinnati, closed because of constant

The Raging Wolf Bobs
Opposite page, located at Geauga Lake, The Raging Wolf Bobs was built in 1988.

The Big Dipper
Opposite page lower left, this classic woodie was built in 1926 and completely overhauled in 1980. It is located at Geauga Lake.

Double Loop
Left, built in 1977 at Geauga Lake, the Double Loop gets its name from its twin vertical loop the loops.

The Beast
Right, from the top of the first lift you can catch a glimpse of The Beast's famous 540-degree covered helix tunnel.

flooding. Most of the attractions, including the ginko trees lining the Coney Mall, were transplanted from the old park to this section of Kings Island.

The Beast (1979)

It took three years to design and construct this wooden coaster, which is America's longest at 7400 feet. Built on 35 densely wooded acres, the riding time is 4 minutes, 30 seconds, with two lifts. The first is 135 feet high with a 45-degree angle drop; the second is 141 feet high with a long steady drop of only 18 degrees that builds into a speed of 64.77 miles per hour before entering a 540-degree helix tunnel.

The Beast
Right, the 135-foot first hill of The Beast at Kings Island dives underground into a dark tunnel.

Vortex
Opposite page, Paramount's Kings Island's Vortex was constructed in 1987.

Vortex (1987)

A steel coaster designed by Arrow Dynamics that turns riders upside down six times. It has two vertical loops, one double corkscrew, and one boomerang. Riding time is about 2 1/2 minutes to cover the 3200-feet-long track.

King Cobra (1984)

This was America's first "stand-up" looping roller coaster. Designed by Togo, Inc., this steel coaster is 2210 feet long and reaches a top speed of 50 miles per hour. It features a 360-degree vertical loop that is 66 feet high and a 540-degree horizontal loop that thrusts riders nearly parallel to the ground.

King Cobra
Right, this $3 million stand-up coaster at Paramount's Kings Island gets its name from the snake-like 360-degree vertical loop and a horizontal loop in its steel track.

The Fastest Roller Coasters in North America

Speed isn't everything, but it certainly gets your heart beating. While The Desperado and Steel Phantom may be the fastest coasters, reaching speeds of 80 miles per hour, there's still a lot to be said for tights curves and high drops; the small yet classic wooden Giant Coaster at Arnold's Park in the Lake Okoboji region of Iowa may not be fast, but the corner that slingshots you out over the lake may be one of the most exciting coaster thrills anywhere. Still, no matter how you look at it, here are the fastest coasters in North America.

Top Speed	Coaster	Material
80 mph	The Desperado	steel
80 mph	Steel Phantom	steel
73 mph	Rattler	wood
72 mph	Magnum XL-200	steel
70 mph	The Screamin' Eagle	wood
70 mph	Viper	steel
68 mph	Great American Scream Machine	steel
66 mph	The American Eagle	wood
65 mph	The Beast	wood
65 mph	Hercules	wood
65 mph	Mean Streak	wood
65 mph	Mindbender	steel
65 mph	Ninja	steel
65 mph	Orient Express	steel
65 mph	Rebel Yell	wood
65 mph	Shockwave	steel
65 mph	Texas Cyclone	wood
63 mph	The Twister	wood
62 mph	Colossus	wood
62 mph	Texas Giant	wood
61 mph	The Racer	wood
60 mph	Cyclone*	wood
60 mph	Drachen Fire	steel
60 mph	Gemini	wood & steel
60 mph	Kumba	steel
60 mph	The Loch Ness Monster	steel
60 mph	Shock Wave	steel
58 mph	Thunder Road	wood
58 mph	Toronado	wood

* Built in 1927, the Cylcone has to be the fastest roller coaster of its age that is still operating!

The Racer (1972)

This coaster is generally acknowledged as having revived the interest in American wooden coasters. Designed by John Allen, this was originally a racing coaster with twin tracks straight out-and-back. Now one of the trains has been reversed so that it runs backward. The tracks are each 3415 feet long and the ride takes approximately 2 1/2 minutes, reaching a top speed of 61 miles per hour.

Adventure Express (1991)

Arrow Dynamics designed this 2963-foot-long mine train-type coaster with two lifts, which are 63 feet and 42

feet high. During the 2 1/2-minute ride, the train travels at 35 miles per hour through four themed tunnels.

Top Gun (1993)

A 2352-foot-long suspended coaster designed by Arrow Dynamics. This is a 1-minute, 30-second, 51-miles-per-hour ride that has a high point of 78 feet.

Top Gun
Above, riders travel below the track on the suspended Top Gun coaster at Paramount's Kings Island, with cars moving at up to 51 miles per hour.

Cedar Point

PO Box 5006
Sandusky, Ohio 44871-8006

This park, on the banks of Lake Erie, first opened in 1870. It is particularly known for its roller coaster lineup with more coasters than any other park in North America. The first coaster to appear at the Point was the Switchback Railway in 1892. Since that time this park has contained almost every type of coaster. During the 1950s, the last of the old coasters were dismantled as part of a park revitalization program that essentially cleared the way for today's coasters.

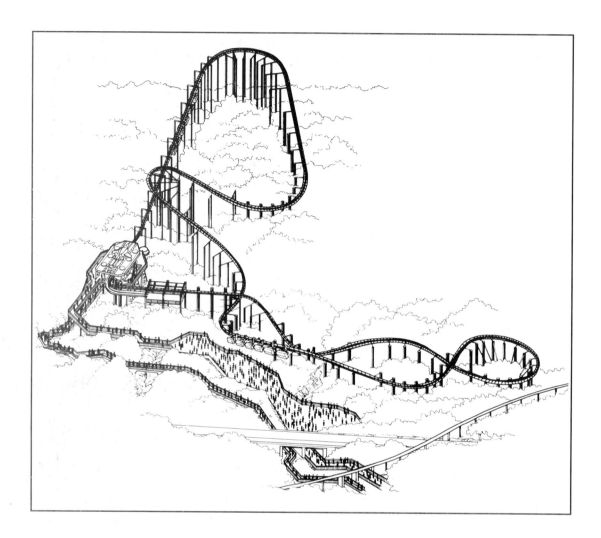

Top Gun
Above, artist's rendering of the suspended steel coaster track that uses 660 tons of steel in its 2300 feet of track.

The Blue Streak
Opposite page, the Blue Streak is Cedar Point's classic woodie, built in 1964.

The Blue Streak (1964)

Built by the Philadelphia Toboggan Company, this is the oldest coaster in the park. It is a fast and hilly, straight out-and-back. It takes only 1 minute, 45 seconds to cover the 2558-foot-long track at a top speed of 40 miles per hour. The first drop is from 78 feet and at an angle of 45 degrees. The loading station is located on a curve, rather than a straight section like most.

Cedar Creek Mine Ride (1969)

One of the first runaway mine train-type rides designed by Arrow Dynamics to go into operation. Its steel track is 2540 feet long with a lift height of 48 feet. This coaster is relatively tame during its 2-minute, 42-second run.

Wildcat (1970)

The Wildcat has fast, sharp turns and brightly colored cars, which hold only four passengers each. This makes the rider fee l a bit more independent, adding even more excitement to the experience. Tight curves, frequent dips, and the rumble of wheels and gusts of breeze created by other cars as they pass around you accent the feel of the ride. It is an overlapping and interlocking figure-eight metal track configuration by Anton Schwarzkopf. At a height of 50 feet and 1837 feet in length, the ride lasts for 1 minute, 25 seconds.

Cedar Creek Mine Ride
Above, built in 1969 for Cedar Point, this is a classic runaway mine train type of coaster.

Corkscrew (1976)

The world's first triple-looping coaster (two helical curves and a 360-degree vertical loop) by Arrow. At 2050 feet in length with an 85-foot-high lift, the ride takes 2 minutes, 15 seconds. It gains a speed off the first hill of 48

miles per hour that slows to 38 miles per hour within the eye of the corkscrew. And for those who would rather observe, the corkscrew offers a great view as it rumbles over the main pathway.

Gemini (1978)

A unique combination of wood and steel, this coaster was the world's tallest and fastest when it first opened. Designed by Arrow, this is a racing coaster with twin parallel tracks in a figure-eight configuration. It is 3935 feet in length and speeds up to 60 miles per hour in its 2-minute, 20-second running time. A 125-foot-lift hill with a 55-degree slope begins a quick, smooth ride, which remains the most popular at Cedar Point.

Corkscrew
Above, built in 1976 for Cedar Point, Corkscrew gets its name from the corkscrew turn and vertical loop.

117

Iron Dragon (1987)

Cars are suspended below the track as they soar through S-curves and spirals, swinging out between the trees due to the forces of gravity. Two chain lifts and several dips take passengers from treetop heights to skimming just above the surface of a lagoon. A final tangle of track pulls riders through a pretzel-knot loop shrouded by mist. This is an Arrow design with two lifts of 76 feet and 62 feet that enable the train to reach 35–40 miles per hour. It takes approximately 2 minutes to cover the 2800-foot-long track.

Magnum XL-200 (1989)

A traditional out-and-back but made entirely of steel, the XL-200 was designed by Arrow Dynamics with an $8 million price tag. It is listed in the *1990 Guinness Book of World Records* as the fastest coaster with the longest drop. The first hill climbs 205 feet above the ground and plunges 194 feet, 8 inches, allowing the train to reach speeds of 72 miles per hour. The second hill drops riders from 157 feet and curves just in time to avoid Lake Erie. Along the way

Iron Dragon
Above, Iron Dragon is a steel suspended coaster built in 1987. Cedar Point's Corkscrew is at right in the background.

Gemini
Opposite page, Gemini is Cedar Point's classic woodie twin-track racer built in 1978.

Magnum XL-200
Above, Magnum XL-200 was built in 1989 for Cedar Point. With speeds up to 72 miles per hour, it is one of the world's fastest coasters.

The Mean Streak
Above, the Mean Streak is a classically styled woodie coaster, built in
1991 for Cedar Point.

there are also three tunnels with special sound and lighting effects. The track is 5106 feet long and the ride time is around 2 1/2 minutes. Also worth noting is the first drop at 60 degrees, making it as steep as any in the world.

The Mean Streak (1991)

The world's second tallest wooden coaster at 160 feet features a 52-degree, 155-foot first drop. The second of twelve hills is taller than most at 124 feet. Designed by Curtis D. Summers and constructed by the Dinn Corporation, this 5427-foot-long oblong-shaped course is traced three times in 2 minutes, 20 seconds. Weaving in and out of the structure, the train can reach a top speed of 65 miles per hour.

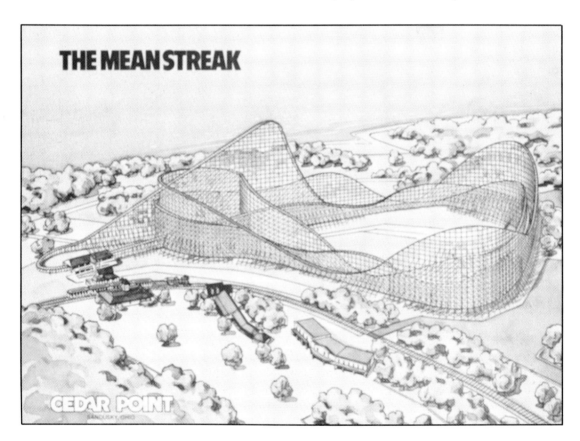

The Mean Streak
Above, layout of the giant Cedar Point woodie.

Raptor (1994)

This inverted steel coaster was designed by Bolliger & Mabillard as the world's tallest, longest, and fastest of its kind. From a lift of 137 feet the train drops 119 feet at a speed of 57mph. The 3790-foot-long ride takes 2 minutes, 16 seconds.

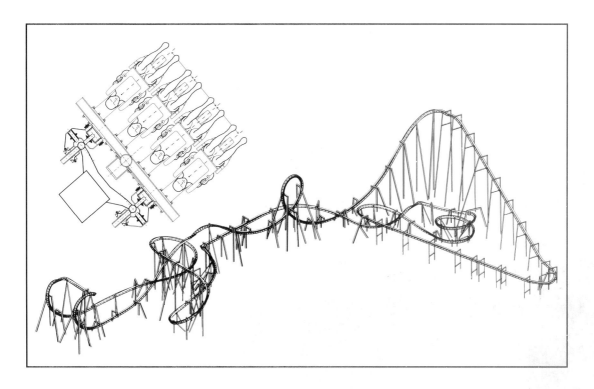

Raptor
Above, layout of the steel-tube inverted Cedar Point coaster built in 1994.

Oklahoma

Frontier City
11601 N.E. Expressway
Oklahoma City, Oklahoma 73131

This small park is themed as an 1880s frontier town and contains all of the usual elements of a traditional amusement park.

Silver Bullet (1979)
This 1942-foot-long coaster found its home here in 1986 after appearances at the Texas State Fair and Jolly Roger Park. Designed by Anton Schwarzkopf, the lift is 83 feet high, which gives the train a 55-mile-per-hour speed into the single loop. Total ride time is 1 minute, 15 seconds.

Wildcat (1968)
Moved here in 1991, this was the last coaster designed by National Amusement Devices. Originally located in Kansas City, this woodie was reconfigured to include a splashdown finale similar to Disneyland's Matterhorn. Sta-

tistically, the 2653-foot-long ride has a 75-foot-high lift, a 65 foot drop, and reaches speeds of 50 miles per hour during its 2-minute run.

Nightmare Mine (1977)
A completely enclosed roller coaster ride.

Oregon

Enchanted Forest
8462 Enchanted Way SE
Turner, Oregon 97392

After seven years of construction this fantasy park opened in August 1971.

Ice Mountain Bobsled (1982)
Designed by Roger Tofte and Dave Windows, this 2000-foot-long steel coaster is an original with an undulating, turning course down a mountainside. The 2-minute ride includes two lifts.

Pennsylvania

Dorney Park
3830 Dorney Park Road
Allentown, Pennsylvania 18104

One of the largest and oldest family owned and operated amusement parks in the country. It includes a water park as well.

Thunderhawk (1924)
Designed by Herbert Schmeck of the Philadelphia Toboggan Company, this 2767-foot-long out-and-back starts from an 80-foot-high lift and weaves its way through the trees of a picnic area during its 1-minute, 20-second run.

Lazer (1986)
This double-looping steel coaster was designed by Anton Schwarzkopf as a portable model. It has a 90-foot

lift and a top speed of 50 miles per hour. The 2200-foot-long track is covered in 1 minute, 30 seconds.

Hercules (1989)

This wooden coaster is unusual in that it begins with a 95 foot lift followed by a 148 foot drop. Curtis D. Summers designed this with the help of the terrain. The track length is 4000 feet and has a top speed of 65 miles per hour.

Lakemont Park

700 Park Avenue
Altoona, Pennsylvania 16602

The park opened in 1894 and is believed to be the home of the oldest roller coaster still standing.

Leap-the-Dips (1902)

Designed by E. Joy Morris, it is the only remaining "side friction figure-eight," which was very popular from about 1900 to 1920. It is believed to be the world's oldest standing coaster. It stands 48 feet tall at its highest point and has a series of gentle slopes along its 1980 feet of track. Considering that this type of ride had essentially become obsolete by the beginning of the 1920s, it is truly remarkable that one has survived. Efforts are currently underway to restore and make it operational once again.

Skyliner (1960)

A wooden roller coaster originally built by John Allen and the Philadelphia Toboggan Company. It was moved to Lakemont Park in 1986 and completely refurbished by Charles Dinn.

Conneaut Lake Park

R.D. 4 Box 283
Conneaut Lake Park, Pennsylvania 16316

This is an old traditional lakeside amusement park.

Blue Streak (1937)

This famous coaster was designed by Ed Vettel and is

especially noted for its unique "camel humps"—a series of three dramatic hills that occur in breathtakingly quick succession on the "out" side of the ride's 2900-foot-long circuit. The wooden structure has a lift hill 78 feet tall and takes 2 minutes, 5 seconds to ride. It is also well known for its "Skunk Tunnel" named in recognition of the numerous times that a coaster train has met a skunk or two in the tunnel that begins the ride, to the mutual dismay and lasting impression of all parties involved.

Knoebels Amusement Resort
RR 1, Box 317
Elysburg, Pennsylvania 17824

Referred to as Pennsylvania's largest free-admission amusement park.

Phoenix (1947)
Originally designed by Herbert Schmeck, this wooden out-and-back was moved here in 1985 from San Antonio Playland ('Rocket') by Charles Dinn. The 2-minute, 10-second ride has a 2300-foot-long track, a 78-foot-high lift, and a top speed of 45 miles per hour.

Whirlwind (1984)
A steel corkscrew designed by Vekoma that was moved here from Playland Park, Rye, New York, in 1993. To make room, the Jet Star was sold to Morey's Pier in Wildwood, New Jersey.

Hersheypark
100 West Hersheypark Drive
Hershey, Pennsylvania 17033-0866

Hersheypark opened in 1907 and personifies the clean, green playground escape that Milton Hershey designed for his hard-working chocolate factory employees. The park is located in a town with history as rich as its chocolate. Tree-lined streets, wide open spaces, and services were created to meet the resident's every need. Today, the town's quaint country atmosphere, inspiring beauty, and many attractions make Hershey a treasured vacation spot.

Soooperdooperlooper
Above, this Hersheypark ride lives up to its name with numerous loops along its steel-tube track.

73 Comet (1946)

This wooden coaster was designed by Herb Schmeck, built by the Philadelphia Toboggan Company, and replaced the Wildcat coaster. Although still a wood structure, the 3360-foot-long track was replaced with a steel track in 1978. The riding time is 1 minute, 45 seconds, and the train can reach a top speed of 50 miles per hour from a first lift of 78 feet.

Soooperdooperlooper (1977)

Designed by Anton Schwarzkopf, this was the first steel loop coaster to be located on the East Coast. The 2614-foot-long track has a lift hill of 70 feet and one vertical loop 57 feet in height. Riding time is 1 minute, 30 seconds.

Trail Blazer Coaster (1974)

A runaway mine train type with steel track, 1874 feet long, designed by Arrow Dynamics.

Sidewinder (1992)

Designed by Vekoma, this coaster is a steel boomerang type. The train is pulled backward to the top of a nearly vertical eleven-story tower, then released going 55 miles per hour into a butterfly section and one vertical loop. The train comes to rest momentarily at the top of another tower before making the same trip again—only backward!

Dutch Wonderland

2249 Route 30 East
Lancaster, Pennsylvania 17602-1188

Located in the heart of Pennsylvania Dutch Amish country, this amusement park opened in 1963.

The Sky Princess (1992)

This 2000-foot-long wooden out-and-back was designed by Custom Coaster, Inc., and installed in just four months. It has a lift of 55 feet, speeds of 40 miles per hour, and lasts for 90 seconds.

The Sky Princess
Below, aerial view of The Sky Princess at Dutch Wonderland. The coaster was built in 1992.
Mike Rieker

Jack Rabbit
Right, Kennywood's Jack Rabbit is one of only two coasters in the United States featuring a double dip. This coaster has been voted by Roller Coaster Fever magazine as one of the top dozen coasters in the country.

Thunderbolt
Above, the last drop is the steepest and fastest on Kennywood's classic 1968 woodie.

Kennywood
4800 Kennywood Boulevard
West Mifflin, Pennsylvania 15122

The park opened in 1898 and was designated as a National Historic Landmark in 1987, with beautiful gardens, fountains, and shade trees. Kennywood is rich in roller coaster history. Today there are five coasters; three wooden and two steel.

Jack Rabbit (1922)

In 1921, one of America's top coaster firms, Miller and Baker, was hired to design a new high speed coaster. John A. Miller designed the $50,000 coaster by taking advantage of a ravine on the edge of the park and thereby using less lumber. A new system of wheels under the track was implemented to allow for the creation of a 70-foot-high double dip. In 1947, a tunnel after the first drop was removed and the original trains were replaced with ones built by Andy Vettel's uncle, Ed Vettel of West View Park. The entire wooden coaster is 2132 feet long with a 70-foot-high lift.

The Racer (1927)

The park's original was built in 1910 as a wooden twin-track racing coaster, which was the world's largest at the time. It did not have wheels under the track, so dips and curves had to be gentle. The new Racer had wheels under the tracks, which permitted banked curves as well as curves on the dips. In his design, John A. Miller, of Miller and Baker, included a reverse curve so the train that started on the right side of the loading platform would finish on the left side. The length of the track is 2250 feet and it has a lift of 72 feet.

Thunderbolt (1968)

Designed by Andy Vettel, this ride has a 95-foot-high lift and is 2887 feet long. It was built around and incorporated the first and last drops and a tunnel of the old Pippin (1924–1967), which was designed by John A. Miller. The Thunderbolt is unusual in that it starts with a drop into a ravine and does not reach the first lift until the ride is half over. This coaster is also well known for its 90-foot final drop.

Laser Loop (1980)

A steel loop coaster by Intamin, using the flywheel method for a catapulting force, which propells the train out of the station to 55 miles per hour in just 4 seconds. At 850 feet long and 140 feet high, the train makes its return to the station backward.

Laser Loop
Above, the Laser Loop at Kennywood trains jet out of the starting station going from 0–55 miles per hour in 4 seconds. This giant vertical loop gave the ride its name.

THE WORLD'S BIGGEST, FASTEST ROLLER COASTER

STEEL PHANTOM

Kennywood
...Roller Coaster Capital of the World

Steel Phantom (1991)

Using the existing terrain, Arrow Dynamics designed a coaster for Kennywood with several elements that have become synonymous with the steel coaster. The 3000-foot-long track includes a twisting first drop from a 160-foot-high lift that leads to the second hill's drop, which has been described as "the thrill of a lifetime." Taking advantage of the natural topography, this drop is the world's longest at 225 feet bringing the train to a world's record for speed—80 miles per hour! This is followed by four inversions, a vertical loop, boomerang, and corkscrew. All of this action occurs within 1 minute, 45 seconds.

Steel Phantom
Opposite page, built in 1991, Kennywood's Steel Phantom is the world's fastest coaster—tied with The Desperado at Buffalo Bill's Wild West Resort in Las Vegas, Nevada—with a top speed of 80 miles per hour.

Zippin Pippin
Left, a classic woodie built in 1915, Zippin Pippin is still thrilling riders today at Libertyland.

Tennessee

Libertyland
940 Early Maxwell Boulevard
Memphis, Tennessee 38104

Located in the center of Memphis at the Mid-South Fairgrounds, this park opened in 1976.

Revolution (1979)
One of the steel double corkscrew coasters designed by Arrow Dynamics with an additional vertical loop that is 75 feet high. It takes 1 minute, 20 seconds to ride the 1565-foot-long coaster.

Zippin Pippin (1915)
Built by the National Amusement Device Company of Dayton, Ohio, this is one of the oldest operating wooden roller coasters in North America and is said to have been a favorite of Elvis Presley. The ride first opened in 1915 in the old East End in the Overton Square section of Memphis, but was brought to the old fairgrounds park in 1923 and re-built at a cost of $45,000. At this time its travel flow was changed to a figure-eight. It has a maximum drop of 70 feet and a length of 2865 feet, and great care is taken to replace its wood every seven years to help preserve the structure.

Opryland
2802 Opryland Drive
Nashville, Tennessee 37214

In the town known as Music City, USA, it is understandable that Opryland would build its reputation on live entertainment. Opening in 1972, this park is also the site of the Grand Ole Opry, which helps earn its nickname of "the home of American music."

Wabash Cannonball (1975)
A corkscrew coaster that races through two giant loops while traveling a 1200-foot-long track at 50 miles per hour. Designed by Arrow, its highest point is 70 feet.

Rock'n'Roller Coaster (1972)

A 2000-feet-long mine train type coaster with two lifts.

Chaos (1989)

This 2620-foot-long coaster by Vekoma International is described by Opryland as the first of its kind in the world. Completely enclosed, Chaos combines traditional roller coaster thrills with state-of-the-art audio and visual technology to give a sense of motion, sight, sound, and touch.

Wabash Cannonball
Below, built in 1975, Opryland's Wabash Cannonball shares little but name with the old steam train of yore.

Texas Giant
Left, everything's big in Texas—especially the roller coasters. The Texas Giant at Six Flags Over Texas runs over nearly a mile of track with top speeds exceeding 60 miles per hour.

Dollywood

700 Dollywood Lane
Pigeon Forge, Tennessee 37863-4101

This is a unique theme park providing "Homespun Fun" amidst the rustic charm and natural beauty that is Dolly Parton's Smokey Mountain heritage.

Blazing Fury

A mild indoor roller coaster ride through a burning town filled with surprises. This ride is a modern scenic railway.

Thunder Express (1971)

Originally built by Arrow Dynamics in 1971 for Six Flags over Mid-America, this coaster was moved to Dollywood in the 1980s. This is a 2500-foot-long runaway mine train-type roller coaster that races over the mountains, weaving through some of the Smokies' most beautiful backwoods.

Texas

Wonderland Park

PO Box 2325
Amarillo, Texas 79105-2325

This park was first opened in 1951 in the city park on land leased from the city under the name of Kiddyland. Business grew fast and in 1967, the amusement park was incorporated under the name of Wonderland.

Texas Tornado (1985)

This coaster is a double-loop steel structure 80 feet tall and 2050 feet long. An unusual-looking coaster, this was the first designed by O. D. Hopkins Associates, Inc. It has been referred to as a "Traver" experience due to its fast paced course, which includes a 200-foot-long tunnel 13 feet under the ground.

Six Flags Over Texas

PO Box 191
Arlington, Texas 76010

Located midway between Dallas and Forth Worth, the original Six Flags park opened in 1961. Its name was chosen for the six flags that have flown over Texas during the past. Originally, it was to be named "Texas Under Six Flags," but as the parks planners put it, "You know how we all feel about Texas, and Texas ain't never been under nothing." Thus it became Six Flags *Over* Texas.

Texas Giant (1990)

This is the world's third tallest wooden coaster at 143 feet. The 4920-foot long track begins with a 137-foot first drop at a 53-degree angle giving it a top speed of 62 miles per hour. This 2-minute ride was designed by Curtis D. Summers of Cincinnati and contains twenty-one drops, probably because this was his twenty-first wooden coaster design.

Judge Roy Scream (1980)

This is a classic wooden out-and-back designed as a family-oriented ride—in other words, exciting but not terrifying. It is 2500 feet long with a 65-foot-high lift and can attain 53 miles per hour during its 2-minute run.

Shock Wave (1978)

This steel coaster by Intamin and Anton Schwarzkopf was the first to feature back-to-back loops. At the top of the 116-foot-high lift, the track curves gently before plunging toward the base of the first loop, which it enters into with a force of 5.9 G's at 60 miles per hour. It only takes about 2 minutes to cover the 3500-foot-long track.

Flashback (1989)

A steel boomerang with a vertical loop designed by Vekoma. The train is pulled up a 125-foot-tall tower and then released to follow the track before stopping at the top of a second tower and then returning backwards.

Runaway Mine Train (1966)

This 2400-foot-long coaster was the first of its kind. It was designed by Arrow Dynamics to give passengers the sensation of being aboard a mining ore train that had gone out of control. There are three lifts, the tallest of which is 35 feet high, and at one point the train travels through a tunnel under a lake.

Shock Wave
Above, the train climbs the lift hill for the big drop at Shock Wave at Six Flags Over Texas. In the background looms the famous double loop.

Astroworld

9001 Kirby Drive
Houston, Texas 77054

The park opened in 1968 under the ownership of Judge Roy Hofheinz and derived its name from the inspiration of the nation's space program. In early 1975, the park was sold to the Six Flags Corporation.

Texas Cyclone (1976)

Designed by William Cobb, this coaster is modeled after the famous Cyclone in Coney Island. It has a 93-foot-high lift and can reach a top speed of 65 miles per hour while coasting over the 3180-foot-long track. The first drop at a 53-degree angle is one of the steepest on any coaster.

Excalibur (1972)

This original roller coaster of the park is a tubular steel track type designed by Arrow Dynamics. It has an 80-foot-high lift with a 60-foot drop reaching a top speed of between 35–40 miles per hour. Originally called the Dexter Frebish Roller Coaster, the name was changed in 1981.

Greezed Lightnin' (1978)

A shuttleloop coaster featuring an elliptical 360-degree loop. Riders are propelled from 0–60 miles per hour in 4 seconds, circle the 80-foot-high loop, then surge up a near vertical 70-foot-tall incline before repeating the same ride backward.

XLR-8 (1984)

A hanging steel coaster designed by Arrow Dynamics. It takes 3 minutes to cover the 3000-foot-long track, which has a first lift of 81 feet. This is one of the first successful suspended coasters following "The Bat" (1981), which was the prototype in Cincinnati.

Ultra Twister (1986)

This ride was moved from Six Flags Great Adventure and opened at Astroworld in 1990. Designed by Togo, Inc., this unusual steel coaster is 1181-feet-long and has a lift of 96 feet. It can reach 43.5 miles per hour during its 1 minute, 40 seconds, through a forward run with one spin rotation and a backward run with a two spin rotation.

Texas Cyclone
Above, the Texas Cyclone at Astroworld is modeled after the famous Cyclone at Astroland in New York's Coney Island.

Texas Giant
Opposite page, the huge first hill stands more then fourteen stories tall. Cars reach 62 miles per hour down the first drop.

Viper (1981)

A single-looping steel coaster created by Anton Schwarzkopf that was moved to the park in 1989 from Six Flags Over Mid-America.

Batman The Escape (1987)

Originally located at Six Flags Magic Mountain, then at Six Flags Great Adventure (1990–1992), the Shockwave has relocated with a new name. This is the only stand-up looping

Ultra Twister
Above, a new concept in coasters, the Ultra Twister cars run with a tube-like caged structure.

Greezed Lightnin'
Opposite page, the massive vertical loop at Astroworld was built in 1978.

Avalanche
Above, built in 1988, Avalanche at Kings Dominion is a trackless roller coaster designed to give riders the feel of a free-moving bobsled ride.

coaster designed by Intamin in North America. It is 2300 feet long, 90 feet high, and achieves a top speed of 55 miles per hour while entering the 66-foot-high vertical loop.

Fiesta Texas
PO Box 690290
San Antonio, Texas 78269-0290

This park opened in March 1992, and is a partnership between subsidiaries of the USAA insurance company and Opryland USA, Inc. Its focus is on live musical productions emphasizing the history, culture, and music of Texas.

Rattler (1992)
Designed by John Pierce & Associates and built by the Roller Coaster Corporation of Texas, this mammoth coaster is built around a limestone quarry and includes tunnels within the quarry walls. It opened with four world records: the tallest wooden coaster structure at 180 feet, 6 inches; the longest first drop of any woodie at 166 feet, 4.5 inches (resulting in a gravitational pull of 3.5); fastest woodie, reaching a top speed of 73 miles per hour; and the steepest first drop of a wooden coaster at 61.4 degrees. The entire ride takes 2 minutes, 15 seconds, covering 5080 feet of track.

Utah

Lagoon
PO Box N
Farmington, Utah 84025

This park opened on July 15, 1886, under the name Lake Park. In 1896, the resort was moved 2 1/2 miles inland to its present location and the name was changed to suit its new location on the banks of a 9-acre lagoon.

The Roller Coaster (1921)
Designed by John Miller, this is a traditional wooden coaster that is 2500 feet long with a high point of 70 feet. It can reach a top speed of 45 miles per hour. In 1953, a fire at the park destroyed the front of the coaster, but it was soon rebuilt.

Fire Dragon (1983)

A steel double loop designed by Anton Schwarzkopf. This ride is 85 feet high, 2850 feet long, and can achieve 55 miles per hour during its 1-minute, 45-second run.

Rattler
Above, the giant lift hill of the Rattler under construction at Fiesta Texas in 1992.

Virginia

Paramount's Kings Dominion
PO Box 2000
Doswell, Virginia 23047-9988

In 1975, the people of Kings Island opened this park and in 1983, Kings Entertainment Company (KECO) was formed, consisting of Kings Dominion, Carowinds, Kings Is-

Anaconda
Right, a one-of-a-kind giant steel coaster, Anaconda at Paramount's Kings Dominion throws riders for a loop six times and is the only looping coaster in the world with an underwater tunnel.

Shockwave
Above, the $3 million Shockwave was the first stand-up coaster on the East Coast. Built in 1986, it is located at Paramount's Kings Dominion.

Rebel Yell
*Above, the classic twin-track racer woodie Rebel Yell was built in 1975
and is located at Paramount's Kings Dominion.*

The Grizzly
Above, running over 3150 feet of track, The Grizzly at Paramount's Kings Dominion ranks among the favorite of the American Coaster Enthusiast Club.

land, and Canada's Wonderland in Toronto. Currently, KECO owns Kings Dominion, Carowinds, Great America in Santa Clara, and 20 percent of Canada's Wonderland. In 1992, KECO was sold to Paramount Studios.

Shockwave (1986)

This is a tubular steel coaster in which riders are secured in a standing position. It is 2210 feet long and reaches a top speed of 50 miles per hour, featuring a 360-degree vertical loop that is 66 feet high and a 540-degree horizontal loop that thrusts riders nearly parallel to the ground. Shockwave was designed by Togo, Inc., of Japan.

Rebel Yell (1975)

A wooden twin racing coaster, each track is 3368 1/2 feet in length. The first of twelve hills is 87 feet high and the top speed is 65 miles per hour during its 2-minute, 15-second run.

The Grizzly (1982)

This is an old-fashioned classic wooden coaster with a lift hill of 87 feet. The 3150-foot-long track is a 2-minute, 20-second ride.

Anaconda (1991)

Designed by Arrow Dynamics, this steel coaster takes riders for a loop six times. From a 130-foot-high lift over a lake, the train plunges 144 feet into a tight underwater tunnel, pops back out and into the first of several loops. The length of this coaster is 2700 feet, featuring the only butterfly configuration in the United States. It has a top speed of 50 miles per hour.

The Hurler (1994)

Designed by International Coaster, Inc., this 3157-foot-long woodie is themed for the "Wayne's World" section and is identical to the one at Paramount's Carowinds.

Busch Gardens, The Old Country
Marketing Department
One Busch Gardens Boulevard
Williamsburg, Virginia 23187-8785

Opening in 1975, this park is owned and operated by Busch Entertainment Corporation, one of the Anheuser-Busch Companies. Its theme links the early American heritage of nearby Colonial Williamsburg with its European roots, featuring eight authentically detailed hamlets.

The Big Bad Wolf
Above, the Wolf is a suspended coaster at Busch Gardens, The Old Country, that is designed to feel as though it is out of control.

The Big Bad Wolf (1984)

A 2800-foot-long hanging coaster designed by Arrow Dynamics. The 3-minute ride includes two lifts of 50 feet and 100 feet, the second of which brings the suspended trains to the top of a cliff before they dive 80 feet toward a lake. At this point the train reaches a top speed of 48 miles per hour just before being whipped to the left to avoid slapping the water.

The Loch Ness Monster (1978)

The first tubular steel coaster with interlocking loops, designed by Arrow Dynamics. The first drop is 114.2 feet at 55 degrees. The speed during this drop accelerates from 12 to more than 60 miles per hour in just 2 1/2 seconds, resulting in a G-force of 3.5. Between the two loops there is a tunnel containing a spiraling track 40 feet in diameter. The entire track is 3240 feet long and the ride lasts 2 minutes, 10 seconds.

Drachen Fire (1992)

Drachen is German for dragon, which is an appropriate name for this wild coaster that was designed by Arrow Dynamics. The brightly colored blue steel track reaches 150 feet in height and 3550 feet in length as it challenges passengers with six inverted elements: three corkscrews, a bat wing, and a "cutback" that will rotate the cars 180 degrees inside a loop. Top speed is 60 miles per hour. This coaster is also the first to include strip lighting on the train itself, which provides for an incredible visual effect at night.

Washington

Puyallup Fair
PO Box 430
Puyallup, Washington 98371

Because this coaster is part of the Puyallup Fair, it only operates two weeks a year.

Roller Coaster (1935)

The original layout by John Miller was destroyed by fire in the 1940s. Walter Leroy then redesigned the coaster in 1950 with a 55-foot-high lift and a double-out-and-back course, 2650 feet in length. The 2-minute ride was also re-configured to accommodate original Prior and Church Trains, the only ones of their kind still in operation.

Canada

West Edmonton Mall
#2872 170th Street
Edmonton, Alberta, Canada T5T 4J2

West Edmonton Mall is a huge complex consisting of recreation, entertainment, and retail. The mall was built in three phases, each opening between 1981 and 1985. Phase II included an indoor amusement park called Canada Fantasyland, which now is home to an incredible steel triple-looping roller coaster. This mall has been listed in the *Guiness Book of World Records* as the largest shopping center in the world.

Mindbender (1985)
This is the world's largest triple-looping coaster and is completely enclosed. The 4198-foot long track has a first drop from a height of 145 feet and the train can reach a top speed of 65 miles per hour. Designed by Anton Schwarzkopf.

Upper Clements Park
PO Box 99
Clementsport, Nova Scotia, Canada B0S 1E0

This Nova Scotia park includes the last coaster completely designed by the late William Cobb.

Tree Topper (1989)
Cobb's wooden out-and-back uses the hilly terrain to its advantage as it weaves around the trees for 1 minute, 15 seconds. The entire track is 1400 feet long, has a lift of 60 feet, and reaches a top speed of 35 miles per hour.

Canada's Wonderland
PO Box 624
Maple, Ontario, Canada L0J 1E0

The Loch Ness Monster
Left, the Monster loops in and out of its own track at Busch Gardens, The Old Country. It reaches speeds up to 60 miles per hour.

This is Canada's largest theme park. It opened in May 1981, just outside of Toronto.

Dragon Fyre (1981)
This steel coaster was designed by Arrow Dynamics, and contains a double loop and a corkscrew.

Mighty Canadian Minebuster (1981)
A large wooden coaster, 3828 feet long and 90 feet tall designed by Curtis D. Summers.

Wilde Beast (1981)
A wooden double out-and-back 3150 feet long also designed by Curtis D. Summers.

Skyrider (1985)
This is a tubular steel coaster in which riders are secured in a standing position. Designed by Togo, Inc., it features one 360-degree vertical loop.

The Bat (1987)
Designed by Vekoma, this coaster turns riders upside down six times in less than 1 minute. It has a boomerang with one vertical loop. It is 875 feet long and has two towers of 125 feet in height.

Vortex (1991)
A suspended steel coaster designed by Arrow. While swinging from side to side as it floats over the ground, the train can reach speeds of 55 miles per hour.

La Ronde
Ile Notre-Dame
Montreal, Quebec, Canada H3C 1A9

This is a traditional amusement park that is located on an island. It opened in 1968, and today features rides, shows and a water park.

Le Monstre (1985)
A huge 3990-foot-long wooden twister with lots of action. The double-track coaster was designed by William Cobb, and at 132 feet in height, is the fifth tallest woodie

Amusement Ride "Boomerang"

Vekoma international bv

in North America and is the tallest of the dual-track coasters. The twisting layout crosses itself eighteen times.

Le Boomerang (1985)

Designed by Vekoma, this steel coaster turns riders upside down six times in less than 1 minute. Riders are first pulled backward up to the top of a nearly vertical eleven-story tower. The train is then released and attains 50 miles per hour, goes through a boomerang and a vertical loop, then heads up another nearly vertical eleven-story tower where the trip begins again—backward!

Le Super Manage (1981)

A smooth tubular steel track corkscrew also designed by Vekoma.

Marineland

7657 Portage Road
Niagra Falls, Ontario, Canada L2E 6X8

This park combines marine life shows, animal petting areas, and a handful of rides including the unusual Dragon Mountain.

Dragon Mountain (1983)

Designed by Arrow Dynamics, this multi-inversion steel coaster begins with a 186-foot lift that drops the train 50 miles per hour into a descending double loop. The 5500 feet of track covers 30 acres and includes 1000 feet of tunnels. The climax of this 3-minute ride is a unique bow-tie loop.

Index